THE POCKET RENOVATOR

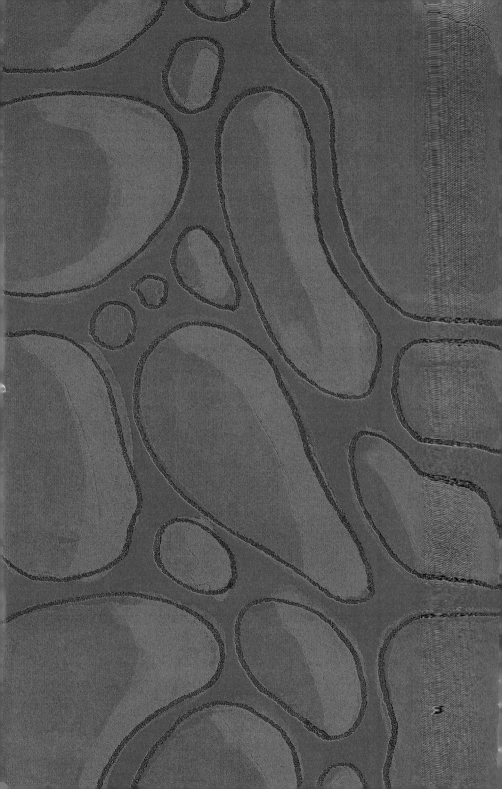

ACKNOWLEDGMENTS

IT WOULD NOT have been possible to write this book without help from knowledgeable friends and colleagues who answered our many questions along the way. A huge thank-you to the following: Charles Muse, Jason Travelstead, Alex Carey, Jim Hanley, Peter Olney, Judith Malcom, Diana Mathias, Seamus Fairtlough, Jay Potash, Nicholas Penfield, Christine Witker, Steven Troup, Julie Williamson, Brewer Schoeller, Maureen Footer, George Grzic, Kent Medowski, Friday Abernethy Weihe, Priscilla O'Neil, Holly Bruning, Heather Bushnell Mock, Lily Malcom, Lulu Kleinbeck, Lela Williams, Kyra Borré, Jenny Raymond, and Courtenay Palmer.

Many thanks as well to Mary Ann Buckwald, Vicky Esposito, Cristina Infante, and George Marshall Peters at Pamela Banker Associates; and to the Writers Room for providing a quiet oasis.

A special thank-you also to Kathleen Jayes at Rizzoli and to our agent Claudia Cross.

Last but not least, David Banker and William Mullins have been encouraging, informative when having their brains picked, and yet again have proven themselves to be all-around excellent guys.

CONTENTS

INTRODUCTION

A FEW YEARS AGO, my mother and I cowrote a book titled *The Pocket Decorator*. It was a book born of necessity. I had started working at her interior design firm and found that despite growing up surrounded by breakfronts, bergères, and batiks, I still wasn't sure what all these things were called, and I wished I knew more about their history and uses. And so an idea was born: *The Pocket Decorator* was the book I wished I had had when I started decorating.

After we finished writing *The Pocket Decorator*, I felt like I knew a thing or two about decorating. That was until I decided to renovate my studio apartment. Suddenly, it was back to square one. Discussing my future built-in desk and bookshelves with a cabinetmaker, I was frustrated when he asked what profile to use on the shelves and I wasn't sure about the correct word for what I wanted (it was bullnose).

And so began *The Pocket Renovator*. Again, my mother and I worked together, with the help of many knowledgeable colleagues, to make this a useful resource for any remodeling or building project. We included chapters on bathrooms, building construction, cabinet-work and built-in furniture, interior layouts, kitchens, preparing for a project, and the vital systems in a house, as well as information on green materials, having a safe and healthy house, financing, and real estate transactions. And, like before, we grouped everything alphabetically by subject to allow you to look something up even if you don't know the proper name for it.

This isn't a book that will tell you how to install a bathtub or fix a plumbing leak. This is a book that will give you the practical information and array of options to be able to ask the right questions and make informed requests of architects, interior designers, contractors, subcontractors (such as plumbers and electricians), and salespeople at home-supply stores. Flipping through *The Pocket Renovator*, you might get ideas you hadn't considered before, such as having copper countertops or using environmentally friendly materials. If you're looking at a house to buy, this book will be useful in understanding how the house works and in considering any improvements.

This book will also provide you with the vocabulary you need for a project. When traveling to a place where they speak a different language, I always have a moment of satisfaction once I've figured out how to ask directions—which quickly dissipates once a helpful local starts answering and I have no idea what he or she is saying. Similarly, architecture, interior design, and construction have their own language, and being able to speak it in conversation (and read plans!) should help immensely with navigating a building or renovation project. This book will help you become proficient in the language, so that you know a vent pipe from a supply pipe.

Since writing the first book, I've fixed up and moved out of a studio apartment in New York, moved into and out of my husband's bachelor pad, and now reside in the country with him in an old house that offers many opportunities for improvement. Through all this moving and improving, I've been constantly reminded that having a house that is stylish, comfortable, and suits your needs is essential to being happy in the space. I've learned that it's helpful to live somewhere for a while before making any changes, to get a feel for how the space works and what your priorities are. I also now know that the fanciest, most expensive appliances are not always the best, and that sometimes just replacing a shower curtain pole and a light fixture is all that a bathroom really needs.

This book documents my own learning curve and satisfies my curiosities about construction, renovation, and the different parts and pieces of a house that make it comfortable. I feel lucky to have a coauthor/mother who has such a wealth of information. I also am lucky to have had the opportunity to work with our talented illustrator George Marshall Peters. We hope this book is a useful tool for you in creating a space that is comfortable, stylish, and exactly what you want.

—*Leslie Banker*

preparing
for a project

1

LIVING THROUGH A RENOVATION is dusty, messy, and generally unpleasant. If possible, stay somewhere else while your house is being renovated. But since moving out is not an option for most, do what you can to make the experience as painless as possible.

Try to seal off the work area with plastic and tape and have a clean area where you sleep. If your kitchen is being worked on, set up a makeshift kitchen area somewhere else, with a coffeemaker and mini-fridge. Be sure to protect existing floors so they don't get scratched, and cover any carpeting so that dust doesn't settle into it. Once the floors are finished, insist that workers and everyone else coming or going through the house take off their shoes or put on paper booties over their shoes before entering. Before work begins, protect or carefully store any hardware, such as doorknobs or light fixtures that you want to reuse.

The *budget* can be a source of stress in a project of any size. It's not difficult to decide how much money you can spend—what is difficult is keeping the project within that budget. To determine how much a building, renovation, or decorating job will cost, get estimates at the outset for everything. If the estimates start adding up to more than your budget, the scope of the project should be changed. This might mean buying a less expensive sofa, deciding not to use marble countertops, or refinishing the bathtub instead of replacing it.

Some work may include additional costs. If you order kitchen cabinets that go up to the ceiling and can only be installed if you take out an existing soffit, then you better know when you order them whether you can afford to take it out. The soffit might have air ducts or water pipes in it; until you get an estimate on all the work, you can only guess how much it will cost.

Remember to save some money for accessories and smaller items. Whether the project is redecorating a living room or remodeling a kitchen, the smaller items will make a big difference in bringing style and a personal touch to the mix. Also, as described below, it's a good idea to allow some money for contingencies; if you don't end up using it, the extra funds will be a bonus at the end of the project.

Capital improvements are an upgrade to the property. When you sell a property, the cost of improving it is typically subtracted from the profit you made on the sale. For example, if you buy a house for $300,000, spend $50,000 fixing it up, and sell it for $500,000, then for tax purposes your profit will be $150,000 and not $200,000. It's important to retain all documentation of capital improvements; this includes bills and proof of how you paid them.

Capital improvements must be changes that will stay with the house after you leave it. These include installing a central air-conditioning system, replacing the windows or exterior siding, upgrading the electrical system, building an addition, finishing a basement, or redoing the kitchen. An accountant can advise on what is considered a capital improvement. One hopes that the costs of such improvements will be all or partially recovered when the property is sold—in many cases, these improvements add value to the property.

Change orders are something to avoid if you're trying to keep a construction project on schedule and within budget: a contractor sends a change order when the original plans for the project change and something new needs to be done or ordered. Sometimes it's impossible to avoid changes—you might never know, for example, that a plumbing line has to be replaced until after a project has been bid and the work begun. However, it's best to plan as much as possible before a project gets underway. If you decide after the project has been bid that you want to have plaster skimcoated walls you will get a change order from the contractor to authorize the additional work and expense.

Contingencies are things that might happen, and if you're starting a sizeable building or renovation project, be sure to set aside money for this. It is generally recommended to allow for about 10 to 15 percent over the original cost estimates. While your design team should do everything it can to bring the project in on budget, sometimes there are surprises. Problems like asbestos remediation, electrical wiring issues, or a termite condition might not be apparent until the walls are opened up and the project is rolling.

While everyone wants to finish a project on time, bad weather or backordered goods may also hold up a job. You should make an effort to keep plans on schedule by evaluating what is beyond your (or anyone's) control, and what can be acted on. For example, you can't control bad weather, which will hold up exterior construction in particular, but you can plan your construction around hurricane season.

The *cast of characters* is the design team that any sizeable construction or renovation project requires, which can include an architect, interior designer, contractor, and subcontractors such as plumbers and electricians. The scope of the project and how much you want to do yourself will determine who you need on your team. Whether you're hiring architects, interior designers, or contractors, it's advisable to ask people you know for recommendations and to interview a few candidates; there's no better referral than someone you trust telling you she would hire her architect again if she had to. You can also ask to see completed projects for a firsthand look at the work of a candidate. When viewing a project by a potential architect, interior designer, or decorator, focus on the design of the space; when looking at a project by a potential contractor, scrutinize the workmanship (for instance, whether tiling is installed neatly and towel bars are level).

There should be a contract or letter of agreement between you and anyone you hire to work on a project. It's important to be clear about what you want and outline precisely your expectations for the job.

The key players in a renovation or building project include the following:

ARCHITECTS design buildings. There are two parts to what an architect does: one is to design the space, and the other is to make sure the structure is sound and complies with building codes. An architect should be able to help you navigate zoning and permit issues, find a general contractor, and oversee various parts of a project. You will need an architect for any substantial renovation or building project.

If you are thinking of buying land and building from the ground up, it's a good idea to take an architect with you to any site you're seriously interested in before you purchase it. An architect will be able to assess whether the site is good for building and will know about utility hookups and other issues.

Architects have to be licensed in the state they are working in and sometimes specialize in areas such as green design or restoration. While an architect's professional qualifications and area of expertise are important, whether or not you communicate well with your architect is also key. The architect should understand what you want and listen to you.

ENGINEERS design a building's structural, mechanical, and electrical systems. Mechanical systems include the heating and cooling systems. Often mechanical and electrical engineers will consult on a project and provide a design to meet performance criteria for the building set by the owner or the architect.

A structural engineer might be consulted on issues such as how to install a stone veneer onto an existing wall, or how a floor can support heavy fixtures such as a big bathtub. If a load-bearing wall is going to be moved, a structural engineer will figure out how to redistribute the weight that it is supporting. Fixing a failing foundation in a house also requires a structural engineer. For new construction, a civil engineer will typically advise on the drainage of a property.

EXPEDITERS shepherd the plans for a building project through the local governing agencies to get the proper permissions and permits. The expediter acts as a middleman between the architect or contractor and the building department. An expediter isn't always used; it's more common to employ an expediter in a city than in rural areas.

GENERAL CONTRACTORS are builders who translate the architect's, interior designer's, or client's vision into reality, hiring subcontractors such as carpenters, electricians, and masons. A contractor should be hands-on, keeping a building project moving forward, scheduling subcontractors, overseeing the work they do, and ensuring that all the materials and supplies are onsite when needed. The contractor must carry insurance and the proper licenses as required by the state that the project is in.

When comparing estimates, make sure each contractor is pricing out all the same specifications: if one includes custom cabinetwork and the other doesn't, then just looking at the bottom line won't be a fair comparison. Pay attention to what is, and isn't, included in a contractor's estimate—will kitchen appliances, doorknobs, and such items be additional? Try to get start and end dates in writing and establish deadlines for phases of the project. Also set up a payment schedule that's mutually agreeable. Ideally, the payment should be tied to the phasing of the job, so that as each step of the project is completed a payment is made. A percentage of the final cost should be held until the end of the job.

It's possible to contract a job yourself, especially if it's a small project or one that you are doing slowly, over time. This means that you hire the subcontractors and schedule and oversee the work. Bear in mind that this takes time and some expertise. While it can save you money, it might end up costing more if mistakes are made.

INTERIOR DESIGNERS are responsible for the planning and design of interior spaces. They have undertaken a formal education to learn skills such as space planning and the preparation of drawings, and in certain states, they are certified to practice. An interior designer can plan renovation projects that won't change the engineering or structure of a building, and they are familiar with building codes and systems, such as heating and cooling. The terms interior designer and **DECORATOR** are often used interchangeably, but they are not the same thing. The decorating of a space includes the choice of window treatments, trims, floor covering such as rugs or wall-to-wall carpeting, and the selection of furnishings and accessories. Decoration only pertains to the surface of rooms, whereas the scope of interior design goes deeper and includes designing built-in furniture and working with construction plans. Design firms often say that they do both "interior design and decoration."

KITCHEN AND BATH DESIGNERS focus specifically on the design of these two rooms. If you are fixing up a kitchen or a bathroom, this designer can help to plan the space, select and order the appliances, and organize the installation. Some kitchen and bath designers work in a retail environment, while others operate independently, meaning they are not affiliated with a particular store or brand. Designers working with a particular brand or store will focus on the products it carries.

OWNER'S REPRESENTATIVES are consultants hired by the owner of a property to oversee a construction project. Typically, an owner's representative is hired in commercial construction projects, but they are also brought in for some large-scale residential projects as well. The owner's representative coordinates and remains in constant contact with the general contractor, engineer, architect, and interior designer on a project. A representative helps with contract negotiations, acts as the eyes and ears for the owner at site meetings, handles the requests for payments, reviews any change orders, and generally ensures that the project is going as planned.

PROJECT MANAGERS oversee the business end of the project for the general contracting company. In some big construction firms, the duties are divided, with a site supervisor at the job site every day and a project manager who is in charge of hiring subcontractors, reviewing and paying bills, and ordering materials. A project manager typically works on several projects at once and won't be onsite every day.

SITE SUPERVISORS work for the general contractor and are onsite daily to oversee a project. In small to medium-sized companies, the contractor and site supervisor may be one and the same. Larger contracting companies have a number of site supervisors, each assigned to oversee and run a project. If an interior designer or an architect is overseeing the construction, then that person should be in constant communication with the site supervisor.

SUBCONTRACTORS specialize in a particular area of construction; they include electricians, plumbers, masons, and so on. There are numerous types of subcontractors, from people who do roofing to glaziers who supply, cut, and install glass. If you are working with a general contractor, he or she will hire and supervise the subcontractors; for smaller projects, or projects you choose to contract on your own, you will hire and supervise them.

Compare a few estimates before settling on hiring one subcontractor. Consider, too, the full scope of a job. You might hire a cabinetmaker to build and install a new bookcase, but that estimate probably won't include painting or electrical wiring to light the bookcase. As always, make sure anyone you hire has insurance and the proper licensing required by the state or city.

Legal review of general contractor and architect's contracts should be done before you sign the papers. A lawyer can help translate and explain any clauses that you don't understand and can bring to your attention any relevant laws. For example, in some areas there are laws allowing subcontractors to file a lien against your property if the general contractor doesn't pay them.

Over-improving is something to watch when planning to renovate a property. Basically, you should not put more money into a property than you can get out of it when you sell. Have a vision of what your property should be worth and don't exceed this in improvements; this might mean using laminate flooring in the kitchen instead of new solid hardwood, for example. Before setting out on a renovation or building project, make sure you understand the real estate market in your area. If you need to sell your house for $400,000 to get back all the money you put into it, but the average price of comparable houses in the neighborhood is $300,000, then it's going to be difficult to make the sale.

These days, the kitchen gets a huge amount of attention and upgrading as people compare their Sub-Zero refrigerators and Viking stoves like skiers comparing the hottest gear. In general, money put into upgrading a kitchen will be recovered entirely or at least partially in the resale value. But this might not be the case if a kitchen is improved beyond what the local real estate market supports. Some also argue that potential buyers like a house without an improved kitchen, so that it can be fixed up to their taste.

A *punch list* details all the little things that need to be done to finish a construction project; if the paint on the front door is scratched, the cabinet knobs haven't been screwed in, the window shade in the library is crooked, or the wood floor has a dent in it, these are all items for the punch list.

The end of a construction project can be frustrating—you're dying for it to be over, and yet all these little things remain undone. The last payment to a contractor is usually made after the punch list items are finished to your approval.

Zoning code and building permits are a fact of life for any substantial construction project, and getting all the necessary approvals takes time and money. Navigating the zoning and permitting processes can be quite complicated.

BUILDING CODES regulate the construction and design of buildings. Local building departments issue building permits based on the local codes. Building codes vary from state to state, so it's difficult to generalize about them. For example The Building Officials and Code Administrators International (BOCA) and the National Fire Protection Association (NFPA), among other organizations, publish general sets of codes that states adopt and then alter as they see fit. A building code may, for example, dictate the minimum height that a ceiling can be and the safety precautions for electrical systems. Because building codes are a complicated matter, it's important to work with architects, contractors, and subcontractors who are familiar with the local regulations. On larger projects, typically the architect will be in charge of adhering to the building codes.

Sometimes in renovation work, building department officials will require that certain aspects of an older building be "brought up to code." This usually pertains to life and safety issues, such as smoke detectors or electrical wiring.

BUILDING PERMITS are issued by local building departments to ensure that structures adhere to the local building code. As a general rule, if you alter the plumbing, electrical, mechanical, or structural systems, you will need a permit. Also, any demolition or new structures will most likely require permits. Not having the proper permit means you could be in violation of the building code and subject to fines.

There are different types of permits, including general building, electrical, plumbing, and mechanical systems permits, to name a few. Generally, before a permit can be issued, construction plans, which show all the changes to be made, have to be approved by a few local boards, which might include a historic district commission, an architectural review board, the department of public health, or a zoning board. The architect usually finalizes the plans and files them with the building department; an expediter, who helps procure permits, may be hired to see the plans through this process. The time it takes to get a permit issued varies from town to town. Once a building department has reviewed and accepted the plans, it issues the permit to the contractor or a subcontractor hired to do the work.

It's an architect's responsibility to know the scope of the project and what permits will be necessary. Contractors and subcontractors should also know which permits are required by a project, but if you have any questions, talk to your local building department to find out what permits, if any, are necessary. If a project is done without the proper permits, typically the property owner as well as the contractor are liable. Homeowners can get permits for work they plan to do themselves, and how this works varies from area to area. Sometimes, the board of directors or managing agent in charge of an apartment building will require that the owner of an apartment submit plans for a renovation to them for review before they go to the building department for a permit; in cities like New York, this is common.

A **CERTIFICATE OF OCCUPANCY,** also known as the **"C OF O,"** is issued once the building department is satisfied that building code requirements have been met. After construction is finished, building inspectors must visit the site to make sure that everything was completed according to the approved plans. Usually, any other agency, such as a department of health or a historic district commission that had to okay the plans for a building permit to be issued, will also have to sign off on the finished work. Legally, you can't live in a building that doesn't have a certificate of occupancy. However, temporary certificates of occupancy can be issued so that you can move into a building before the final C of O is issued.

ZONING is overseen by local planning departments and regulates how a structure can be used—for example, whether a property is for commercial or residential use, or how tall a building can be. Before doing construction work that will change a building's **FOOTPRINT,** or the area that it sits on, first check with the local planning department to make sure your plans are in line with local zoning ordinances. In some situations, a **VARIANCE** is granted allowing a structure to depart from the local zoning code; this may be necessary, for instance, to build a house that is closer to a property line than the zoning code permits. An **EASEMENT** is the right to use property owned by another person for a specific use, such as for a path to the beach that crosses someone's private property.

SETBACK refers to the distance from the property line to where your house, deck, or outbuilding (such as a shed) can start. If you don't adhere to the setback determined by your municipality, it could make you move the structure. This is something to look into in the early stages of a building project or when buying a property with an eye to adding onto the house.

TIPS FOR SMOOTH SAILING

Whether you're renovating or building from scratch, there are a number of things you should (or shouldn't!) do to make things run as smoothly as possible:

Do as much as possible before construction begins. Specify and refine plans over and above what you thought you'd have to. Check that every outlet is where you need it, the storage space is sufficient, the correct kitchen appliances are specified, and floor and wall finishes are as you want them. It makes a huge difference to know what you want while the project is still in the planning phase, and it's essential to have a full furniture plan at the earliest stages.

Assemble your design team as early as possible. If you're hiring both an architect and an interior designer, it's important that the interior designer be involved during the planning stages of the project.

Don't change your mind! Once you've accepted a bid from a contractor, changing your mind leads to change orders, and more time and more money being spent. Try to settle on everything before you start construction work.

Learn to read plans (see p. 35) so that you know what you're signing off on.

Don't micromanage. You've done your research and hired the people you thought were best for the job. Let them do their jobs.

Don't pit the architect against the builder, or the architect against the interior designer. Try to work as a team as much as possible.

Be willing to accept a second choice. For example, if the marble sink of your dreams is backordered for six months, think about a plan-B sink that can be delivered more quickly.

Keep in mind that building and exterior work can be delayed due to bad weather—blizzards, hurricanes, monsoons, or just plain old rain.

Be prepared for delays in the delivery of goods, especially if they are imported—things can get held up in customs. Put orders in early, and think about using domestic items if you're trying to avoid delays.

Commit to the project fully and try to attend weekly meetings onsite with the design team. Make sure you, or your interior designer or architect, are available for questions from the contractor or subcontractors.

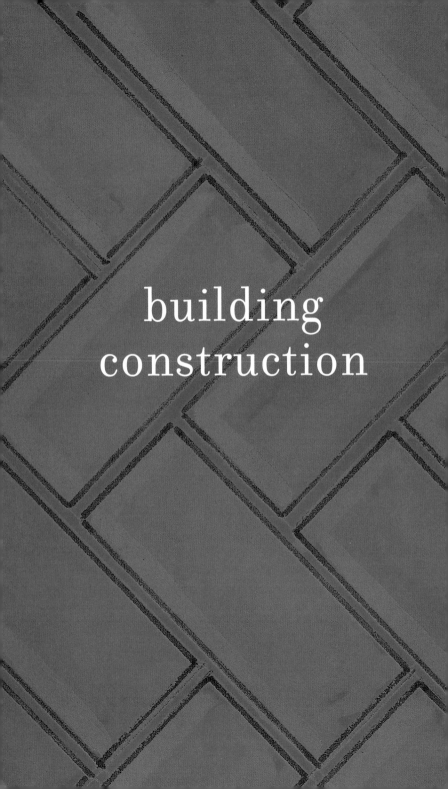

building
construction

2

BUILDING, EITHER FROM THE GROUND UP or renovating, is a major undertaking that often takes more time and money than initially planned. Living through a renovation can be trying as well. The upside is that the final result is a house you love that suits your practical needs and aesthetic sensibilities.

When considering a building project, start by thinking about how you would ideally use the space. Think about your favorite activities and plan accordingly: if you love to cook, make the kitchen your oasis. Also make a list of things that annoy you about the current space that you want to change. If you have an expanding family, make sure there's enough room to grow. With any project, consider making the house as environmentally friendly as possible. And if you are restoring an older house, take the time to do the required research on the style of architecture that was typical of the period. Deciding the direction of the project and your priorities are the initial steps. Then figure out how much money you can spend. It's much more efficient to know generally what you want and have a budget in mind before talking to architects, interior designers, and builders.

Exterior elements, such as the siding on a house, the roof design, and the material covering the roof, do much to determine the look of a building. More importantly, they are also the first lines of defense against sun, rain, snow, and sleet. A new roof or new siding can be an excellent capital improvement; the cost of this improvement should be recouped, or a significant portion of it, when you sell the property, as long as it's still in good shape.

FLASHING is sheet metal used on a roof or an exterior wall to protect the building from water seeping in. It's installed at seams, such as where a chimney meets a roof, where two planes of a roof meet, and around window and exterior doorframes. Different types of metal can be used for flashing. Copper lasts a long time but is also expensive; aluminum is a more economical choice. If the flashing isn't installed correctly, the roof and walls will be prone to leaks. When you're reroofing or re-siding a house, it's important to make sure that the proper flashing is installed to protect the house from water damage.

ROOFING MATERIALS come in a wide variety: thatching with straw or reeds was common hundreds of years ago and is still seen in the English countryside, among other places; medieval churches sometimes were built with lead roofs; and some environmentally friendly designs have turf roofs. When considering the different options, be sure to find out how long each material is expected to last. Remember that climate is a factor in roof material longevity.

If you are redoing the roof of an older house, take into account the original material; whenever possible, retain the character of an old house by maintaining or restoring the original roofing materials.

It's critical that a roof be installed correctly: while the material itself might hold up for fifty years, if it isn't installed well problems might arise a lot sooner. New materials are constantly being developed, but some current standards are detailed below:

ASPHALT SHINGLES are thin pieces that overlap the same way that wood shingles do. They range in color from very dark to lighter shades. Asphalt shingles don't have the architectural pizzazz of other more substantial materials such as slate or cedar shingles, but they get the job done. They last about twenty years and are one of the least expensive choices.

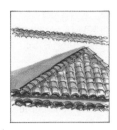

CLAY TILE ROOFS are typical of the Spanish Colonial, Mission, and Mediterranean architectural styles and are often used in conjunction with stucco siding. Tile roofs are also common on Japanese temples, though not typically in the terra-cotta red of Spanish Colonial and Mission styles. The tiles are made with clay or concrete and are fire resistant. They are often semicircular and installed as alternating convex and concave tiles to give the roof a wavy surface. A tile roof is heavy, so it's critical that the building be able to support the weight. It's possible to find salvaged clay tile for a roof, which might be perfect for a restoration project. Clay tiles generally have a lifespan of a few decades or more, depending on the type and the climate where they are installed. In green design, salvaged materials are used when possible, as it's more efficient to reuse materials than to make new ones.

METAL ROOFS are, as the name implies, constructed using thin sheets of metal. Aluminum, steel, and copper are some of the options for roofing. These products generally come with warranties of twenty to fifty years, meaning that, if maintained, they should be expected to last even longer. For installation, the metal is typically screwed into a wood sheathing. Metal roofs come in different styles: some are made to look like shingles, while corrugated metal roofs have ridges running down them. Metal roofs are often popular in places where wood is scarce, like Reykjavik, Iceland. They are also chosen in green design because they can be made with recycled materials and then can be recycled at the end of their life; also, metal reflects heat which can help to cut down on energy costs in hot climates.

SLATE is a beautiful roofing material, typically of a blue-gray color. Slate stone roofs are expensive but last anywhere from seventy to one hundred years or more, depending on the type used. Many late-nineteenth- and early-twentieth-century buildings still have their original slate roofs; in the United States, one well-known example of a slate-roof building is the Pentagon, in Washington, D.C., built in the 1940s.

If you are buying a house with a slate roof, pay extra attention to the roof's condition, as it will be a significant cost to have to replace it. If you are thinking of adding a slate roof to a house, confirm that the structure of the house can support the weight of the stone. Some argue

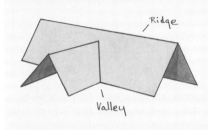

Ridge

Valley

The **RIDGE** of a roof is the high point where the sloping planes meet.

The **VALLEY** of a roof is the low point where the planes meet.

that if you invest in a more expensive roof that lasts a long time, you will save money down the road by not having to replace the roof multiple times. From an environmental perspective as well, longer-lasting roof material is more earth friendly. Artificial slate roofing is available at a lower cost, but while it looks similar and sometimes is made from recycled material, it typically doesn't last as long. For a restoration project, purists will argue that a slate roof should be replaced with real slate, not artificial slate.

WOOD SHINGLES and **WOOD SHAKES** are generally made of cedar. They typically last thirty to forty years; local weather will affect the longevity of the roof. Shakes and shingles are similar, with a few key differences. Shakes are split from a block of wood, whereas shingles are sawn from a block of wood. Shakes typically are thicker and have a more rustic appearance; shingles are smoother and create a more tailored look. That said, there are shakes made with a smooth surface. Both shingles and shakes darken as they weather.

ROOF STYLES do much to determine the look of a building. But no matter the shape of the roof, its purpose is to keep out the elements. In colder areas where there's lots of snow and rain, pitched roofs are advisable.

CUPOLAS are small domes that extend above the line of the roof. A cupola is typically open to the room below, providing light and ventilation. Cupolas were used in classical Roman architecture and subsequently in the styles influenced by it. A wide variety of buildings feature cupolas on the roof, from barns to churches and residential houses. A **BELVEDERE** is a cupola with windows and stairs for access.

FLAT ROOFS are traditionally used in arid regions where shedding water and snow isn't necessary. Despite being called "flat," many such roofs are slightly angled. Pueblo-style adobe houses in the southwestern United States often have flat roofs, and in the Middle East and areas of Asia flat roofs are the norm. Modernist architects, such as the enormously influential Le Corbusier (1887–1965) and Ludwig Mies van der Rohe (1886–1969), frequently employed flat roofs in their designs. Many city apartment buildings and townhouses also feature this style of roof. A flat roof is prone to leaking if it's damaged, however, so it pays to be careful when considering building a deck on top of or otherwise using one.

GABLE ROOFS, one of the most basic roof styles, slope in two directions. Ancient Greek buildings such as the Parthenon and the Temple of Athena Nike originally had shallow sloping gable roofs. These days, houses ranging in style from Cape Cod to ranch and Tudor can have gable roofs. Because it is such a simple design, it is also typically less expensive to build than more complicated ones. The gable is the triangular area of the house beneath the eaves of the roof. There are a few different types of gabled roofs; *front gable* houses have the front door under the gable (as pictured here).

Cross gable roofs have two or more gable rooflines that intersect. A cross gable allows for more complicated layouts in a house. Instead of being confined to a rectangular shape, a building with a cross gable roof can have wings going off in different directions.

Side gable roofs feature the front door under one of the planes of the sloping roof. This is a basic construction for a house and is incorporated in many different styles.

GAMBREL ROOFS are a variation of the gable roof in which each side has a shallower slope over a steeper slope. This type of roof was characteristic of the Dutch Colonial style of architecture in the late nineteenth century during the Colonial Revival. This design is associated with barns and is often seen with dormers—windows that project from a roof. The gambrel roof is similar to the mansard, the difference being that the gambrel roof slopes on only two sides of the building, while a mansard roof slopes on all four sides.

HIPPED ROOFS, also known as **HIP ROOFS,** slope in four directions. The "hip" is the angle formed at the meeting of two sloping sides. This roof is found in a variety of styles, from Georgian to Prairie. Typically, a hipped roof is rectangular with a ridge along the top. A hipped roof in which the four sloping planes meet at a single point is called a **PAVILION HIPPED ROOF.** A **CROSS HIPPED ROOF** has two or more intersecting hipped roofs, much like a cross gabled roof. A hipped roof is thought to withstand hurricanes better than a gable roof, which has only two sloping sides.

A *half hipped roof,* or *jerkin head roof,* is a gable roof with small hipped ends called the jerkin head. This is seen in Bungalow style houses, as well as other designs.

MANSARD ROOFS are hipped gambrel roofs, meaning that the roof has four sloping sides, and each side has a shallow slope over a nearly vertical slope. The steep lower slope of the mansard roof allows for a full attic space. This roof often includes dormers and has a French look to it. In fact, it is named after the

SALTBOX ROOF

French court architect for Louis XIV, François Mansart (1598–1666), who incorporated it into the buildings he designed. The style was popular during the latter half of the nineteenth century, particularly in cities, and is typical of the Victorian row house.

A **SALTBOX ROOF** (above) is seen on the so-called saltbox house typical of Colonial architecture in New England. The house is two stories high in the front and only one story high in the back. The roof is a variation of the gable roof, typically with a chimney rising up through the center.

SIDING is the material that covers the exterior walls of a building. Historically, siding material was almost always locally grown or quarried: in areas where trees were plentiful, wood was often used; where trees were not as abundant, then brick, stone, or adobe were employed. However, as transportation systems improved and it became easier to ship materials, other options were made feasible, like wood shingles in the desert. Still, specific areas have developed particular styles of siding. For example, wood shingles and clapboard siding are typical of the northeastern United States. In the twentieth century, man-made sidings such as aluminum and vinyl became economical and popular choices. The choice of siding does much to determine the character of the house and should be considered carefully, especially for a restoration project. When possible, the original siding on a house should be restored or reproduced, as this helps to preserve the original look. New siding, particularly when it's in keeping with the historical character of the house, can increase the resale value of the property. Siding typically goes over a layer of sheathing, which often is plywood secured to the framing of the house, and a layer of felt paper or house wrap, which protects the structure from water vapor and air infiltration. As with roofing materials, siding materials will have varying life expectancies—it's important to ask about the expected lifespan and maintenance of particular products as you consider them. Some commonly seen types of siding include the following:

BOARD AND BATTEN SIDING is comprised of parallel boards installed with battens, which are narrow strips of wood, over the seams between the boards. Typically, board and batten siding runs vertically. It has a country look that is seen on barns, frontier houses, and in the Gothic Revival style. Rough boards give the siding a more rustic appearance than smooth ones.

BRICKS are made of clay that is molded, dried, and then fired, and have been used in construction for nearly six thousand years. Their standard shape and small size make transporting and working with them easier than stone. This timeless material is used for everything from city buildings to country houses; Hampton Court, the historic palace of Henry VIII in Surrey, England, has a brick exterior, as does Thomas Jefferson's beloved house Monticello, near Charlottesville, Virginia. A brick exterior can be left its natural color or painted. Exterior bricks can also be installed in a variety of patterns, called bonds (see the masonry section on p. 28 for examples). Brick is strong and durable and can last for many decades: remember, in *The Three Little Pigs* fairy tale, after the wolf huffs and puffs, it's only the house made of brick that is still standing.

CLAPBOARD (pronounced "cla-berd") is siding with overlapping horizontal strips of wood that typically are beveled, or tapered, so that one edge is thicker than the other. It is also known as **BEVELED SIDING** or **LAP SIDING**. Clapboard is common on older American

houses, especially in New England; the house where writer Nathaniel Hawthorne was born in Salem, Massachusetts, has clapboard siding. Different styles of clapboard have developed in different regions, so it's a good idea to research the style specific to your area. Clapboard can be painted or stained and sealed. Stain produces a more muted color than paint.

FIBER CEMENT SIDING is a man-made product that is guaranteed for approximately fifty years and can be painted any color. It is made to resemble wood shingles or clapboard siding. Fiber cement siding also comes in flat panels. It is valued in green design for its longevity.

HALF-TIMBERING shows the wood posts for framing the building and the plaster between them. This is typical of the Tudor and Jacobean periods in England, as well as the Tudor Revival style in the nineteenth century, which incorporated elements of the original Tudor look. An extreme example of half-timbering can be seen at Little Moreton Hall in Cheshire, England, built in the mid-sixteenth century (the architect is unknown); the half-timbering gives the house's exterior a wild pattern.

STONE has been used as an exterior material for millennia. Examples of famous stone buildings include Elvis Presley's Graceland in Memphis, Tennessee; the classic brownstone buildings in New York City; and the Great Pyramid of Khufu outside of Cairo in Egypt, which dates from approximately 2600 BC. From cottage to castle, stone is a timeless material. It can be used as a decorative exterior layer of siding, in which a 3- to 4-inch-thick stone veneer is installed over the structure of the building. Alternatively, a wall can be of solid stone, from the interior through to the exterior. Manufactured stone—man-made material that resembles natural stone—is an option as well.

STUCCO is a plaster made with portland cement, sand, and lime that goes on wet, a state known as "plastic," and then hardens into a solid surface. This mixture is applied over wire mesh, called lath, or directly over the wall material. Traditionally, it is applied in three

layers: a "scratch coat," a "brown coat," and a "finish coat." It is typical of dry temperate climates, such as that of the Italian countryside, where wood was not readily available for building. Stucco tends to hold cool air in a building, and so was also preferred in warm climates. Stucco can be found in some wet climates as well, such as England.

The word "stucco" is derived from the old Germanic word *stucki*, meaning "crust." It was used by the ancient Romans, and in traditional Islamic architecture in North Africa and Spain; it is also typical of the Spanish Colonial style, paired with a red tile roof. In Santa Fe, New Mexico, stucco is common and almost always painted or tinted an adobe earth tone to simulate the old adobe clay blocks that houses were historically built with.

Stucco can be painted or have pigments mixed into it for color. Over the centuries, the recipes for stucco have changed, but in general the effect is the same—a textured and durable exterior. Today, a synthetic stucco is available called E.I.F.S., which stands for Exterior Insulation and Finish Systems. It is typically less expensive than real stucco and provides a good amount of insulation for the building. Architects and builders can detail the pros and cons of real stucco versus synthetic stucco, as well as which synthetic stucco products are best for a particular project.

VINYL SIDING is made, typically, to look like clapboard siding. It's less expensive than wood siding and comes in a variety of styles and colors. Vinyl siding has been used since the twentieth century and has grown in popularity over the decades. While it doesn't require painting and as much maintenance as wood siding, it can be prone to denting. Vinyl siding won't age or weather the way real wood does and so isn't as aesthetically pleasing. For a restoration project or any older house, when budget permits the original siding should be preserved or replaced.

WOOD SHINGLES are pieces of wood, typically cedar, with one end thicker than the other. They are used for siding and roofing and are installed so the individual shingles overlap. There are also **WOOD SHAKES** which are similar to shingles but instead of

ACOUSTICS are the characteristics of a room or a building that determine the audibility and quality of sound in the space. Ideally, when you're sitting in the living room, you don't want to hear every step and sound upstairs, or every car passing by outside. An architect or interior designer should be sensitive to this, but it's still a good idea to bring it up. Most houses are laid out so that quiet spaces are near quiet spaces, and loud spaces near loud spaces. Bedrooms generally are grouped together, while living areas and kitchens are positioned near each other. If you're planning on having a screening room, a music practice room, space to rock out in, or having to cope with a bedroom facing a noisy street, do what you can to ensure unwanted sound doesn't come in (or blast out).

Additional insulation can be installed in walls or between ceilings and floors to muffle sound. Walls can be constructed so that studs alternate sides of the wall they are affixed to; this arrangement prevents them from transmitting vibrations through the wall. A double layer of wallboard absorbs more sound than a single layer, and adding a layer of plywood under the wallboard also increases sound absorption. Landscaping, such as a hedge or a row of shrubs, can deflect noise from outside. Wall-to-wall carpeting installed over padding, or even an area rug, absorbs more sound than a bare floor does. Upholstered walls and lined curtains also help cut down on noise.

being sawn from a block of wood like shingles, they are split from one. Shakes typically have a more rustic look and are thicker. Both shingles and shakes can be stained, painted, or left in their natural color, which will weather.

The Shingle style flourished in the late nineteenth century; it started in New England and was adopted around the country. As the name suggests, shingles were the siding and roofing of choice. The architecture firm McKim, Mead, & White designed some of the best examples; many of these houses are in Long Island, New York, and Newport, Rhode Island.

Insulation prevents the transfer of heat or sound from one space to another. It keeps heat inside a house and cold temperatures out, or vice versa. Insulation between walls and floors contains sound in one area, instead of letting the sound vibrations flow through walls and between ceilings and floors. Having a house insulated properly will keep heating and cooling bills down, thus conserving resources. Insulation can be added to foundation walls, hot water pipes, and existing walls. The amount of insulation a house needs depends on the climate and its structure.

Insulation is rated according to its **R-VALUE**, which stands for resistivity value, a measure of its resistance to heat flow. Insulation with a higher R-value offers greater protection against the transferal of heat. A number of different types of insulation are used in building construction. **BATT INSULATION,** which looks like cotton candy, comes in rolls or pads and often has aluminum foil backing. **LOOSE-FILL INSULATION** is blown or poured directly into the spaces in the wall, ceiling, or floor. **RIGID BOARD INSULATION** consists of boards that are, for example, secured to the exterior of a house under the siding. **EXPANDING FOAM INSULATION** is sprayed onto or applied to the interior of walls or used to fill gaps and holes. "Green" versions of insulation are made with recycled content and few VOCs (volatile organic compounds), which are released into the air during and after installation of most insulation and can be toxic. These environmentally friendly products are well worth looking into.

Masonry is construction using stone or brick or similar materials, and a mason is someone who does this work. The word is thought to come from the Old English word *macian*, meaning "to make." Today, the work of a mason is similar to what it was hundreds, even thousands, of years ago. The following are the types and details of masonry work:

BRICKS can be used for the construction of interior and exterior walls of a house, interior floors and exterior paving, garden walls, and chimneys and fireplace surrounds. Mud bricks date back to at least the fourth millennium BC; these bricks were made with a mixture of straw and mud that was molded and then dried in the sun. Mud was also used to hold the bricks together, and a layer of it might have been spread over the walls to create a smooth surface. Traditional adobe construction—which is still used today in the southwestern United

BRICKS

Bricks have different names depending on their position and the face that is exposed in a wall or paving, as follows:

HEADER
the short end
laid horizontally

SHINER
the widest face
positioned horizontally

ROWLOCK
the short end
laid vertically

SOLDIER
the long edge
positioned vertically

SAILOR
the widest face
positioned vertically

STRETCHER
the long edge
positioned horizontally

States—is similar to this ancient method. Fired bricks first appeared in about 3000 BC in Mesopotamia (part of which covers present-day Iraq). During the Roman Empire, bricks were used widely, and brick-making techniques improved.

Bricks come in different grades, which reflect how well they will stand up to freezing temperatures and frequent rain. They are available in colors ranging from the standard red to lighter yellow hues. There are also glazed bricks that have a decorative ceramic coating. For restoration, it is often necessary to source old brick, as new brick will not have the same patina and look of older brick. Bricks used for paving are called **PAVERS**.

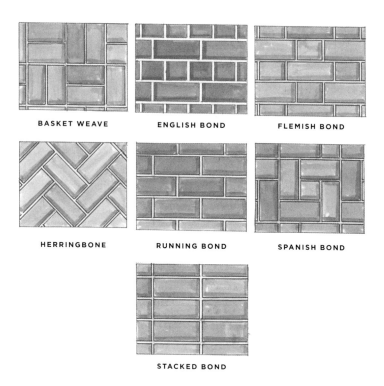

BASKET WEAVE · ENGLISH BOND · FLEMISH BOND

HERRINGBONE · RUNNING BOND · SPANISH BOND

STACKED BOND

BRICK PATTERNS have evolved over many hundreds of years, and builders or architects in specific locations have developed and favored certain ones. The Finnish architect Alvar Aalto (1898–1976), for example, was known to incorporate interesting and unusual brick patterns in some of the Modern buildings he designed—these were riffs and embellishments on more traditional patterns. Some brick patterns are better for paving than for constructing walls, and vice versa, and some are more expensive and labor intensive than others to install. The word "bond" describes bricks that are placed in a repeating pattern; this is done for both decorative purposes as well as strength. It's also possible to lay stones in some of these patterns.

Many patterns have been created over the years; the following are a few commonly seen ones:

BASKET WEAVE has squares of bricks facing in alternating directions; each square consists of two bricks. In the pattern, there are two bricks side by side facing vertically, with two bricks side by side facing horizontally next to them. This is a common pattern in paving areas such as paths, stoops, and patios. The bricks usually have a border, such as a row of stretchers, framing the area.

An **ENGLISH BOND** has alternating rows (called courses) of stretchers, which are bricks laid horizontally on their long side, and headers, where bricks are laid horizontally to expose the short side. This traditional bond is mostly used for walls.

A **FLEMISH BOND** has rows (courses) where the bricks alternate between the stretcher, which is the long side, and the header, which is the horizontal shorter end. The header of one course is centered on the stretcher of the course above and below. This bond is used for walls and, like the English bond, is something you might see on a traditional brick house.

A **HERRINGBONE** pattern is made with rows of bricks forming a "V." This pattern can be made with strips of wood or stone as well. A herringbone pattern in brick is used for paving.

A **RUNNING BOND** is a common pattern for walls and paving. The bricks are laid horizontally with the long side, or stretcher, exposed. The vertical seams between bricks are staggered, which gives the construction strength.

A **SPANISH BOND** is used for paving. It has a more intricate pattern than a running bond or a basket weave. A Spanish bond will give additional pattern and detail to a path or a patio.

A **STACKED BOND** has bricks laid horizontally with their long sides, or stretchers, exposed. The vertical seams line up, giving this pattern a modern look but little structural strength. It can be used either on walls or in paving. A running bond, where the vertical joints between bricks are staggered, is stronger.

CONCRETE BLOCKS come in standard sizes and are a basic building block in the construction of walls. They are used in this capacity instead of, or in conjunction with, a timber frame. Walls are frequently constructed with concrete block in warmer climates, as it holds cool air in a house.

CONCRETE:
FROM ANCIENT ROME TO GREEN DESIGN

Concrete is a Roman innovation and was used to construct famous buildings such as the Colosseum and the Pantheon in Rome. Since concrete starts out in a pliable state and dries solid, it allows for impressive curved forms such as arches and domes. While there is evidence of earlier use of concrete, it was the Romans who improved the recipe and first employed it widely. They discovered that if they added *pozzolana*, a volcanic ash, to the concrete, it would even harden under water. When the Roman Empire declined, *pozzolana* concrete fell out of use, and it wasn't until the nineteenth century that concrete again became as strong and useful as what the Romans had developed.

Today, the many different kinds include reinforced, pre-cast, and low-density concrete. Concrete is used to build everything from skyscrapers to sidewalks and kitchen coun-tertops. In green design, concrete is being made with coal fly ash, a byproduct of coal-fired electricity generating plants. The fly ash makes the concrete stronger and also disposes of an otherwise useless industrial byproduct.

GLASS BLOCKS allow light through but also provide some privacy, as the thickness of the glass distorts the view through it. Glass block first appeared in the 1930s and was often used in Modern architecture. It is a particularly good material for partitions. Standard sizes range from 4½ to 12 inches square. The blocks are typically 3 to 4 inches thick.

MORTAR is the material placed between bricks, stone, or concrete block to bind them together. It is made from a mixture of cement, lime, and aggregate, which are bits of stone or sand. The mortar can affect the look of masonry. If the stones have some distance between them and a strip of mortar is showing, the building will have a more rustic look. A very fine strip of mortar between stones creates a more refined and formal appearance.

REPOINTING is repair work done to the mortar between bricks or stone. Over time, the mortar on a building exterior will become weathered and need to be fixed. In repointing, the old mortar is removed by chiseling it out and new mortar is put in. When a house is being inspected for a potential buyer, the inspector should look at whether any repointing needs to be done.

STONE is durable, comes in myriad variations—from marble to limestone and granite—and has many uses in construction, such as for walls and floors. Traditionally, a house was built with local stone, as it was too difficult to transport large quantities of heavy stone from far away. In certain areas today, such as Bucks County, Pennsylvania, you'll still see many houses with exteriors made of the same type of stone. Today, stone can be shipped more easily, but local stone is still a good option where available. The following detail some examples of stone in construction:

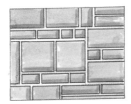

ASHLAR is stone that has been cut to have corners with right angles. It can be laid either in courses, meaning rows, or in a random pattern. (It's opposite is rubble, where the stone has not been cut to any particular shape.)

CRAZY PAVING is made from broken slabs of stone. As the name implies, the stone is all different sizes and shapes, like a crazy quilt, which is made from scraps of cloths sewn together in an abstract fashion. Crazy paving is generally less expensive than installing cut stone. It has a more rustic and whimsical look than ordered stones with squared corners.

RUBBLE is rough stone in irregular shapes. **COURSED RUBBLE** (pictured here) means that the stones are laid in rows, or courses. This creates a rustic look that is a little tighter and more organized than random rubble. Rubble is more likely to be used on a country house than an urban building.

SYMBOLS USED ON PLANS

You should become familiar with several important symbols commonly used on construction plans (in addition, if you see the letters "AFF" it means "above finished floor"):

 DUPLEX ELEC-TRICAL OUTLET: an outlet that fits two separate plugs

 **POCKET DOOR:** a door that slides into a pocket in the wall so that it is concealed when open

 FIREPLACE

 **HALF-SWITCHED OUTLET:** a duplex outlet where one half is controlled by a switch and the other half is not

 QUAD ELECTRI-CAL OUTLET: an outlet that can accommodate four separate plugs

HINGED DOOR: the plan will show the direction the door swings in

R **RECESSED LIGHT FIXTURE**

 INSULATION: the R-value of the insulation will typically be noted. The higher the R-value the more resistant the insulation is to the transfer of heat

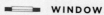 **SLIDING DOOR:** a door with two or more panels that slide open and closed

SWITCH: a wall switch that flips on and off to control lights and such

LIGHT FIXTURE: a ceiling light fixture symbol would have breaks in the line of the circle

 WALL-MOUNTED LIGHT FIXTURE: a wall sconce that is wired directly to an electrical box to the wall

 WINDOW

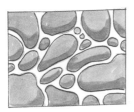

Random rubble is rough stone, which has not been cut, laid in a random pattern instead of in rows. A house with a random rubble exterior has a particularly rustic appeal to it. The pieces of stone vary in size and can be quite large; on the façade of a house, you might see rubble 1 foot or more in length. Because rubble is rounded, it is not commonly used for paving.

Plans are the critical drawings from which a house is built; blueprints are copies of the original plans. When working with an architect or an interior designer, it is important to be able to read plans so that you can check, for instance, that bookshelves are where you want them and that the cabinetwork and closets are all to your specifications. A renovation or building project will go more smoothly if you pay full attention to the plans before the work begins. Read plans to be sure, for example, that there's enough hanging space in closets; you could measure your current hanging space and compare it to what is called for in the plans. Ask yourself if there is adequate storage in the bathroom for towels and cleaning supplies. Is there a place to keep a vacuum cleaner and linens? Where will you place your sound system, TV, DVDs? Think about where you will sit and read, and then make sure there is an electrical outlet nearby for a reading light. Do you have a big beautiful painting? Then check that there's a good wall to hang it on in the new space.

Plans are drawn to scale, meaning that the proportions in the drawing are exactly the same as that of the actual building. A typical scale is a $\frac{1}{4}$ inch = 1 foot; this means that $\frac{1}{4}$ inch in the drawing represents 1 foot of the actual structure. Thus, a room that is 16 by 16 feet will be drawn as 4 by 4 inches in $\frac{1}{4}$-inch scale. The scale used will be noted somewhere on the plan.

A scale ruler is used to draw and read a plan; it is typically one foot long with three distinct sides giving it a long triangular shape. Each long edge of the ruler measures in a different scale. For example, the edge that is in $\frac{1}{4}$-inch scale will have numbered marks spaced a $\frac{1}{4}$ inch apart. These numbers represent the measurement in feet at $\frac{1}{4}$-inch scale.

Plans can be drawn by hand or on the computer; those created on the computer use CAD software, or computer-aided design. The many different types of plans for buildings include: mechanical plans that show the ducting and heating elements like furnaces and boilers; foundation plans that depict foundation walls and major structural elements in the basement; framing plans that detail how the structure will be framed; and roof plans which show exactly how the roof will be built. When building or renovating, some plans to pay particular attention to are the following:

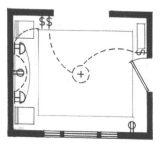

ELECTRIC AND LIGHTING PLANS show all the light switches, outlets, and light fixtures. Switching is something to pay special attention to when planning a new space. This refers not only to the location of wall-mounted switches, but also to which switches control the fixtures. For example, a ceiling fan must have its own wall switch to turn it on and off. You don't want one switch to control wall sconces and also the ceiling fan, or it won't be possible to turn one on without the other. A wall switch at the entry of a room is typically required by building code, and you must decide what will be operated by the switch: will it be the center ceiling light fixture, or a lamp in the far corner of the room? If both are to be switched separately, then a double switch will be required; this will have two separate controls that flip on and off independently.

In a renovation, usually half of every electrical outlet is controlled by a switch and the other half is not. This allows maximum flexibility as to what you can turn on when you flip a switch at the entrance of the room. However, you don't want a bedside light, an electric clock, or a television on a wall switch; electrical outlets near a bedside table are best left manual.

ELEVATIONS are drawings of a vertical surface such as a wall or the side of a building. They include details like molding on the wall. If you are having built-in bookcases made, an elevation drawing shows how they will look. To see how a specific console table will work with a certain size mirror above it, an elevation could be drawn to scale to show how the pieces will look in relation to each other.

FLOOR PLANS describe a single level of a building viewed from above. This includes walls, windows, doors, skylights, and staircases, as well as the ceiling's height and pitch, and overhead elements such as chandeliers. When trying to reconfigure the space in a house, you can take a sheet of tracing paper, lay it over the existing floor plan, and use a pencil and scale ruler to draw in ideas or see how certain changes might work. A furniture plan is made using a floor plan.

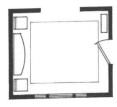

FURNITURE PLANS depict the furniture layout drawn to scale for each level of a building. Though it may seem counterintuitive, a furniture plan should be done while a construction project is still in the planning stages. Until you start placing furniture in the rooms, it won't be possible to know what will fit; you will want to know if your 12-foot dining table will work in the dining area, or that there are outlets for lights in every place you'll need them. Even if you are not doing construction, a furniture plan is always handy when you're moving to a new place. You can measure the furniture that you have and draw the pieces to scale on a sheet of paper. Then, cut the scale drawings of the furniture out and position them on a floor plan drawn to the same scale as the furniture.

NATURAL LIGHT is important to keep in mind when designing and decorating a house. In the northern hemisphere, windows facing the east will warm quickly in the morning. North-facing windows will be the chilliest and have little direct sunlight; however, artists often prefer northern exposure for their studios, as the light is most consistent throughout the day. West-facing windows will heat up quickly in the late afternoon. Windows facing the south will get sun all day, but not as intensely as the east-facing windows in the morning or west-facing windows in the afternoon.

REFLECTED CEILING PLANS show the ceilings as if they were reflected onto the floor. In other words, it depicts the ceiling as if you were a bird with X-ray vision looking through the roof at the ceiling. A reflected ceiling plan details where ceiling-mounted light fixtures will be placed, and where any vents, speakers, or exposed beams are located. With this plan, you can make sure track lighting will be where you want it, and that recessed light fixtures will shine down on the artwork you plan to hang.

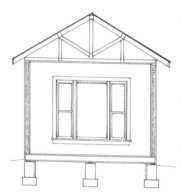

SECTIONS portray a vertical cross section of a building, as if sliced from the top of the roof down to the ground. These can include the details of the cross section of the walls, ceilings, and floors—showing, for example, what type of insulation will be used in construction. A section shows elements and details of the construction that are not necessarily visible on the exterior. When designing built-in furniture, such as a built-in bar, a section might show the under-counter lighting, the interior of the cabinets (drawers and shelves), the panel details on cabinet door or drawer faces, the profile of the edge of the countertop, and the height and thickness of the backsplash.

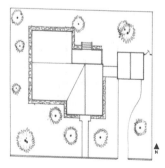

SITE PLANS detail how a house or structure will sit on the property. It's a bird's-eye view of the property depicting where each structure is located and situated—which direction the front door faces, for example. A site plan typically includes the location of utility hookups. It's a good way to consider what rooms in the house will have the best views, and since a site plan shows which direction different rooms will be facing, it can be used to determine how to best take advantage of natural light.

Structural elements are the various components that hold up a building. When talking to architects, interior designers, and contractors, it helps to have a basic knowledge of this terminology. Many houses, especially in cooler climates, have a timber construction, meaning the structure is framed with wood. Softwood, which is from evergreen trees, is used for general construction, while hardwood, which comes from a wide array of deciduous trees, is more often chosen for flooring and furnishings. This is true in part because softwood is less expensive and more readily available than hardwood. Although softwood is relatively softer than hardwood, it is successfully used for framing a building. There are houses where masonry, such as concrete blocks, is used to construct the walls, and this is known as masonry construction. Any changes to a building's structure should be done in consultation with an architect or engineer. Here is a basic rundown of a building's structural elements:

BEAMS are horizontal structural elements that can be made of wood, stone, or metal. The word comes from the Old English word for tree. Joists and lintels (see p. 41) are types of beams. **GIRDERS** are heavy-duty supports for a structure that are also a type of beam.

COLUMNS are vertical structural elements. In ancient Greek and Roman architecture, columns were both decorative and structural, part of the classical orders of architecture that developed in these civilizations. These classical columns are comprised of, from top to bottom, a capital, a shaft, and a base.

PILLARS are a type of column typically made of stone or brick. A column can also be a vertical metal support running through a high-rise building. **POSTS** are another type of column usually made of timber and incorporated in timber framing. A post may support a deck or it may be used in post and beam framing, which was common in houses constructed during the eighteenth and early nineteenth centuries.

The **FOUNDATION** is the base that supports a building. It is at least partially below ground level, or "below grade." The exterior walls of a house are typically supported on the walls of a foundation, while the interior load-bearing walls are supported by elements such as columns and beams. When looking to buy a house, the inspection should include a thorough check of the foundation. Some signs of problems are cracks and shifting in the foundation walls or noticeably uneven floors in the house above the foundation.

FRAMING is the process of creating the structure of a building, like a skeleton, using beams, studs, and other structural elements. In a renovation or construction project, framing is the first step to building new walls, ceilings, or floors. An early framing technique used throughout the eighteenth century, was known as **POST AND BEAM FRAMING;** instead of nails, notches in the posts and beams held the frame together. In the late nineteenth century, lumber in standard sizes became increasingly available and with this **BAL-LOON FRAMING** developed. This type of framing had studs, which are vertical supports for a wall, usually 2 by 4 inches, that extend the entire height of a house running from one story to the next. If you are renovating or restoring an older house built around the turn of the twentieth century, chances are it was constructed with balloon framing. **PLATFORM FRAMING** is common today; instead of having the studs extend the entire height of a house, they are only as long as one floor and are secured to a platform built between the floors that acts as an anchor.

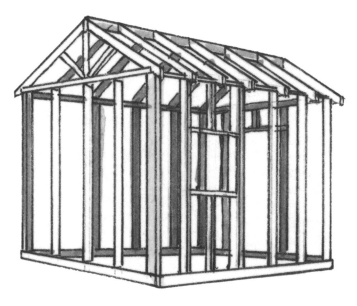

JOISTS are supports for floors and ceilings typically made of lumber. Joists run parallel to each other and are set on their sides, so they are higher than they are wide. Joists are set 16, 20, or 24 inches apart, depending on the size of the lumber and the length of the span the joists are crossing. The word joist is thought to come from the Latin word *jacere* meaning "to lie." Load-bearing walls usually run perpendicular to joists to support them. A problematic joist can reveal itself in the form of a sagging or squeaky floor; this might be an indication of damage to the joists from termites or other insects. Joists also can be weakened if they aren't properly supported to begin with. If there's a problem, it should be possible to have the existing joists reinforced.

LINTELS are horizontal supports that span an opening such as a doorway or window. The word comes from the Latin word *limitaris* meaning "threshold." Lintels are also sometimes called **HEADERS.** The weight, or load, that a lintel must carry and the size of the opening in the wall will determine how big it has to be. Lintels may be either visible or concealed in the wall, depending on the architectural look of the building.

LOAD-BEARING WALLS support weight from above. A load-bearing wall might be placed under joists that need to be supported. If you're planning to move walls around, the load-bearing walls should be identified. It is easier and less expensive in a renovation not to move or alter a load-bearing wall. To move one, you have to replace it with a support such as a column or steel beam; an architect or engineer can advise. Generally, an interior load-bearing wall is supported underneath by another load-bearing wall, or posts—some element to hold the weight. Walls that are not load-bearing are relatively easy to cut into and move around, as they won't affect the structure of the building.

RAFTERS are diagonal timbers that support a pitched roof. They are usually placed parallel to each other and will have specific names

BLOCKING

When hanging items such as bathroom accessories, kitchen cabinets, flat screen TVs, and heavy mirrors onto wallboard, blocking is recommended to anchor them, since wallboard alone is not very strong. Blocking is a piece of wood installed behind the wallboard spanning from stud to stud, so that the nails go into the wood as well as the wallboard. Instead of wood, metal strapping—a strip of sheet metal—can be used as well. The metal is screwed onto the face of the studs before the wallboard goes up. Since the wood (or the metal) goes in before the wallboard, it's important to plan in advance where accessories and fixtures will be hung. If you don't know, ask your contractor or subcontractor to add blocking to any place you think you might want to install something.

To hang heavy items on an existing wall, another option is to use an anchor such as an expansion bolt. This is a screw that fits into a sleeve that is placed in a hole in the wall. As you tighten the screw, the sleeve expands in the hole to create a tight fit. This is not optimal for extremely heavy items, but should suffice for lighter ones such as towel bars.

depending on their position and purpose. A fly rafter, for example, is the rafter in a gable roof that projects beyond the exterior wall. The **RIDGE BOARD** is at the top elevation of a pitched roof and is what secures the rafters.

STUDS, vertical structural elements, are approximately 2-by-4-inch or 2-by-6-inch pieces of lumber. They are typically placed inside a wall at 16-inch intervals as part of the framing in many residential buildings and usually span the height of a wall from floor to ceiling. In a building with multiple stories, studs are as long as needed to span one level of the house and are anchored to a platform between levels, in the area between the ceiling of one level and the floor of the next. When hanging a heavy item on a wall, whether it's a kitchen cabinet or a large mirror, nail into the studs so the weight of the object is properly supported. Additional support in the walls, called blocking, can be added by securing wood boards horizontally between studs.

TRUSSES are a combination of beams, rafters, and other structural elements that create a framework to support a structure like a roof or a bridge, for example, over an open space. There are many different types, each with a slightly different structure. The ancient Romans were known to use trusses in construction, and it is still a standard today.

Walls can be constructed with many different materials. They may be solid brick or stone, or have just a veneer (decorative surface) of brick or stone. An exposed brick wall can make a space feel cozy with its warm color, while a stone wall creates a great rustic look. Walls can also be paneled with wood or covered in plaster. In modern construction, they are often built using drywall, where wallboard is screwed into studs. In the past, however, walls were typically made of plaster over bricks, stone, or strips of wood, which is called lath. A very solid and acoustically sound wall construction would be insulation covered by plywood secured to the studs, with wallboard over everything.

DRYWALL is a method of construction in which panels of wallboard are affixed to the framing of the building. This method was developed as a replacement for plaster, which is typically a mixture of gypsum or lime, water, and sand that is applied as a paste and hardens as it dries. There are a few different types of wallboard. One common type is gypsum board, also called plasterboard, which has a layer of gypsum (a mineral used in making plaster) sandwiched between layers of thick paper. Sheetrock is a trademark for a brand of wallboard, although the name has become widely used for wallboard in general. You'll sometimes even hear it used as a verb, as in: "They are sheetrocking today." Green board is for use in wet areas such as bathrooms;

PREFAB HOUSES

PREFAB, short for **PREFABRICATED,** is a house that is to some degree manufactured offsite at a factory and later assembled onsite.

Some prefab houses arrive preassembled, needing just to be hooked up and secured to the foundation. Others come in kits, with all the pieces cut at the factory and ready to be assembled. There are also prefab houses that arrive partially assembled. With any prefab construction, you still need to build a foundation and have the utility hookups available. The opposite of a prefab house is a custom-built house.

Sears, Roebuck and Company was one of the first companies to offer prefab houses in their catalogues. Between 1908 and 1940, the company sold thousands of prefab houses. Families would pick a house from the Sears catalogue and the mass-produced, precut timbers and pieces would arrive on the local railroad. Prefab houses were also adopted by some espousing modernist ideals. In 1954, the architect, mathematician, and inventor R. Buckminster Fuller patented the geodesic dome, which is available today in kits that are assembled and can be lived in.

Prefab houses can be customized, and they vary in cost. Generally, a prefab house takes less time to assemble than constructing a custom-made house and should be less expensive, since the parts are mass produced. Costs to look into before committing to the prefab option include: buying the land, building the foundation, hiring a contractor to finish the house, transporting the house from the factory, hooking up utilities, building permits or fees, and property taxes.

Today, prefab houses are available in cutting-edge modernist designs as well as the traditional standards. If you're building from scratch, adding a wing, or even thinking of a new outbuilding on your property, it's worth looking into prefab.

blue gypsum board can be covered in a thin layer of plaster, to give the walls the look of being made with plaster. Some gypsum wallboard is made with recycled material and synthetic gypsum, which makes it a good choice for a green building project.

Typically, a wall is framed so that there are studs (vertical supports) to which the wallboard is screwed. The seams between the boards are taped and the screw holes are filled with a joint compound, and then the wall is ready for primer and paint or wallpaper. The standard size of wallboard is 4 feet wide by 8 to 16 feet long. The hollow space behind the wallboard is usually filled with insulation. Both wallboard and insulation come in various thicknesses, which determine how energy efficient and soundproof the wall will be.

These days, most new buildings use drywall construction, as it's faster and much less expensive than old-fashioned plaster. If you're restoring a house built before the 1940s, when drywall came into regular use, you will probably find that the original walls were constructed with plaster. Where possible, it's best to maintain the plaster; however, this is expensive, and in most cases drywall will be used even in an older house that is being restored. Contractors may choose drywall for new walls and ceilings and leave plaster on existing walls and ceilings—this is especially true if the new wall area is large. In this case, the drywall may be covered with a plaster veneer, known as skimcoating, to make it match the appearance of the existing walls.

Applying plaster is messier than installing drywall as it goes on wet and can drip and spill. However, installing drywall is much dustier than plastering.

PLASTER is usually a mix of gypsum or lime, water, and sand that is applied to walls while wet and solidifies as it dries. Plaster is typically spread over framing (where wood studs support the wall), or over masonry walls. A **LATH** is the surface that plaster is applied to; wood slats or wire mesh is commonly used for lath. Mud is a primitive form of plaster seen in the earliest construction of buildings and is still used in developing countries.

It used to be that most houses had plaster walls. Today, with the cheaper alternative of drywall, not much new construction is made with plaster because it is significantly more expensive. But for a restoration or preservation project where the budget permits, plaster would be the appropriate choice, and it is an investment that should last for a long time. Acoustically, a thick plaster wall is better than one constructed of drywall because not as much sound will be heard from one room to another in the house. Also, in situations where a wall has curves, such as arches around windows, plaster produces the best result. Veneer plaster or plaster skimcoating is another alternative, which combines plaster and drywall.

PARGET also refers to plaster, in particular to decorative plasterwork. The Tudor period in England is known for some incredible examples of ornate plasterwork, or pargeting, particularly on ceilings that had a geometric pattern with pendants of plaster hanging down. Plaster also lends itself to decorative painting. Venetian plaster is a decorative treatment that has been applied for centuries, using multiple coats of plaster for a beautiful finish that can have a variety of textures and colors.

VENEER PLASTER, also called **PLASTER SKIMCOATING,** is a combination of drywall and plaster construction. A specially treated gypsum board, called blueboard, is put up and then layered with one or two thin coats of plaster, giving the walls the harder and more uniform surface of plaster construction. This method costs more than regular drywall but is much less expensive than full plaster construction.

Whether you're moving to a new house or have simply decided to spruce up an existing house, the *improvements* that can be made are innumerable, and it can be overwhelming—and potentially bankrupting—to start thinking about them all at once. The first thing to focus on is the systems—the heating, plumbing, electric, and so forth. If there are any repairs or improvements that need to be done to the systems, that should be the first priority. Next is the fun part of fixing up the house, either through complete remodeling or just by changing a couple of things around to make life easier. Usually, landscaping and exterior work can wait until the interior is settled; also, if you're doing work to the interior as well, you don't want people traipsing through your new grass and shrubbery. What follows is a rough rundown of what some improvements entail; more specific and detailed information should be obtained on a case-by-case basis from experienced and licensed contractors and subcontractors.

ADDING OR MOVING CABLE WIRES

When moving into a new house, or just rearranging the furniture in your old house, you'll often find that the cable for the TV and modem isn't where you'd like it to be. In some situations, your cable company may be able to relocate the cable wire, or an electrician can do it for you. Decide where you want the cable to be, then talk to the cable company and/or an electrician about the work.

Ideally, the cable is run so that it's invisible. It can be run inside the walls, but this is only worth doing if you're already planning to repair the walls and repaint. Alternatively, the cable can be stapled onto the surface of the wall just above the baseboard. It can also be run behind the baseboard or under wall-to-wall carpeting next to the tackless—the strip of wood with tacks on it used for carpeting installation. These options should be considered only if the baseboard is being changed or if new wall-to-wall carpeting is being installed. Keep in mind that moving a cable wire is best done before painting.

Of course, the possibility of bringing cable to a house where it doesn't already exist depends on whether a cable company serves the area. If not, satellite television is an alternative. If a company can provide cable service, they should be able to bring the wire to any location in the house.

ADDING OR MOVING ELECTRICAL OUTLETS
Once you've decided where your furniture will go, you might realize that there is no electrical outlet near where you want to place the stereo or a new appliance, for example. If you're installing a new outlet, an electrician can advise on whether it can be added to an existing circuit. If too many outlets are put on one circuit, the circuit breakers will trip regularly, since the circuit is more likely to get overloaded. If you can't add a new outlet to an existing circuit, or if you want a dedicated outlet that is the only one on the circuit, there needs to be space in the main electrical panel for a new circuit, and wires have to be run from the main panel, or a smaller subpanel, to the new outlet. The amount of work this entails depends on the location of the new outlet in relation to the main panel (or subpanel) and also on the construction of the walls.

It's relatively easy to cut into a wall constructed of wallboard to add a new outlet or to move an existing one. The wallboard will need to be patched and painted afterward. With a plaster wall, adding or moving an outlet is more work, as a channel has to be chopped into the wall to run the wires, which creates a lot of dust, and the wall then has to be repaired and repainted. New electrical wires can also be run in wire molding, which is mounted on the surface of the wall. While visually this is not the best option, it is certainly less expensive and easier than cutting up the wall to move wires.

ADDING OR REMOVING MOLDING

Adding molding, such as a baseboard or crown molding, is a relatively simple process that requires securing them to the wall and then repainting or wallpapering the wall. Adding or changing molding can improve the look of a room dramatically and can make the ceiling appear higher. Removing molding requires patching and repairing the wall behind it. Be prepared to repaint or wallpaper the entire wall in either case. See p. 71 for more information on moldings.

CHANGING A COUNTERTOP OR BACKSPLASH

A new countertop or backsplash can give a kitchen a great face-lift. Even if you're not planning on reconfiguring the kitchen layout or the cabinets, you could replace, for example, scratched-up lime-green Formica with something a little spiffier. The expense and the amount of work required depends on the material you use. Some countertops and backsplashes are easier to change than others; laminate should be relatively easy to take out, whereas stone might require more work. If you're changing the countertop around a sink or a cooktop, these will have to be disconnected and reinstalled with the new countertop. More information about backsplashes and countertops begins on p. 107.

CHANGING OR MOVING APPLIANCES

If there's an old range or refrigerator in your kitchen that has seen better days, consider replacing it. In general, replacing an appliance with one that is the same size and has the same requirements for fuel, electricity, venting, or water supply should be relatively easy. If you're replacing a refrigerator, note whether the old model had a water line for ice cubes and chilled water. If not, a plumber will have to install one if the new refrigerator is to have a working icemaker and water dispenser.

Moving appliances from one location to another in a kitchen involves more work and is part of a larger remodeling project. Most appliances need GFI, or ground fault interrupter, outlets for use near water sources. (See p. 163 for more information on GFI out-lets). Moving appliances may also mean reconfiguring plumbing and gas lines.

CHANGING DOORS

If a house has hollow-core doors, you might consider upgrading to solid doors—either flush (flat) or paneled. As long as the new door fits the opening and the doorjamb is measured correctly, it shouldn't require too much effort to install a new one. The doors and doorframe will require painting.

CHANGING HARDWARE

Replacing tired or unattractive doorknobs, cabinet knobs, or pulls can be a great pick-me-up for all rooms in a house. Doorknobs and the plates behind them, called escutcheons, can also be replaced, and, if you really want to go all-out, new hinges can be installed as well. When switching hardware, be prepared to have to touch up the paint, especially if the new hardware covers less of the surface than the old one.

CHANGING WINDOWS

Replacement windows can help to make an older house more energy efficient. While it can be quite expensive to replace windows, more efficient windows can cut down on the amount of cold air, noise, and dirt entering a house. New windows can be installed into existing frames, provided they are carefully measured. If there is rot or other issues in the window frames then the entire frame will have to be replaced, which will entail more work. For added energy efficiency, windows can have low-e glass (see p. 180 for more information on low-e glass). Touch-up painting will be required after installation. An alternative to replacement windows is restoring older windows and adding storm windows for insulation.

PAINTING

A fresh coat of paint is a huge pick-me-up for a house—whether inside or out. Talk with an expert about which products are recommended for a particular situation—for instance, the best type of paint to use for interiors and exteriors will vary. The walls should be properly prepared for painting, and this includes scraping and sanding areas where paint is peeling, filling cracks and holes in the wall with a spackling compound and then sanding the surface, cleaning the walls, and removing hardware plates (such as those for light switches). If the surface of the walls is uneven or bumpy from years of multiple coats of paint, skimcoating the walls with plaster will make the surface smooth; however, this also adds considerably to the cost. Use masking tape to get a clean line at the edge of the area to be painted. A coat of primer should be applied, followed by the chosen paint color. Consider painting the ceiling a color besides bright white, such as a very light shade of the wall color or a contrasting color.

HANGING WALLPAPER

Wallpaper can add great interest and style to a room. It is more expensive than painting, however, due to the cost of the paper and the labor of installation. The walls have to be prepared before the wallpaper is hung, which includes smoothing the surface and coating them with a layer of primer or sizing to help the wallpaper stick. It's possible to hang wallpaper yourself, although it is certainly more complicated than painting: the wallpaper strips have to be hung perfectly straight (a plumb line is used to achieve this), and the pattern of the wallpaper has to line up from strip to strip. Getting the wallpaper on without bubbles and blisters takes some skill, but you'll never learn unless you try it. If in doubt, hiring an experienced paper hanger for the job can mean avoiding expensive mistakes.

Removing wallpaper from a wall entails using a steamer or a chemical paper remover. It's possible, although not advisable, to paint over wallpaper; this should be done with caution, as any irregularities in the surface will show through the paint, and some wallpaper will leech dyes into the paint. Discuss the possibilities and best products to use with a wallpaper hanger or an experienced salesperson at a paint retailer.

OPENING UP OR CLOSING A DOORWAY

In some cases, it's a good idea to close up a doorway and replace it with a wall. This entails removing the door, door casing, and threshold and framing the doorway with studs (the vertical supports for a wall). Insulation is then added, and the wall is closed up on both sides, typically with wallboard or plaster (or brick, or however the surrounding wall is finished). Both sides of the wall will have to be repainted or wallpapered.

To open up a doorway, the same thing happens but in reverse. If there are any plumbing lines or electrical wires in the wall, this means more work to reroute them. If the wall is load-bearing, meaning it helps support the weight of the building, the procedure is more complicated and will require an architect or an engineer to look at it.

PUTTING UP OR TEARING DOWN A WALL

There are two types of walls: those that simply divide a space, and load-bearing walls that divide a space and also support the weight of the structure. Removing a wall that carries no weight is relatively easy, as long as there aren't plumbing lines or electrical wires in the wall; if there are, they would have to be rerouted. Tearing down a load-bearing wall is much more complicated and must be overseen by an architect or an engineer. The weight that the wall is supporting has to be redistributed using other structural elements, such as a steel beam.

Putting up a wall requires framing it with studs, adding insulation, finishing the wall with wallboard or plaster, and finally painting or wallpapering. If the room has molding, such as a baseboard or crown molding, it should be matched and continued on the new wall.

REFINISHING OR PAINTING A WOOD FLOOR

A solid wood floor can be refinished, which involves sanding and then restaining or painting it. Some wood floors with a veneer can be refinished as well, depending on the material. Laminate floors, which have a digital image—wood or stone, for example—covered in a thick protective layer, cannot be sanded; if they are damaged, they must be replaced. To refinish a floor, all the furniture must be removed. Sanding is very dusty work, and you should be prepared to touch up the baseboard or bottom of the wall after you're done. A painted wood floor can be very stylish, and restaining an old floor breathes new life into it.

cabinetwork
and built-in
furniture

3

BUILT-IN FURNITURE MAKES USE of every available inch of space. It can help to organize a room and keep clutter at a minimum, and it meets your requirements exactly: a built-in bookcase can be the same height as the ceiling and precisely as wide as you need it to be. Built-in furniture—from kitchen cabinets to window seats to radiator covers—is an integral part of the architecture and contributes to the character of a house.

People have been building furniture into their houses for centuries. In sixteenth-century England during the Tudor period, you were likely to see built-in settles, which were high-backed benches, as well as long built-in tables. In eighteenth-century American Colonial architecture, the built-in cupboard was typical; recessed into a niche in the wall, it often featured open shelves above and enclosed shelves below. During the Arts and Crafts movement in the second half of the nineteenth century, built-in furniture was an integral ingredient of the architecture.

Carpentry is the broad category of woodwork done by a carpenter. In construction, it is carpenters who build the structure of a timber-frame house. Finish carpentry is the term used for finer work, including making and installing molding such as crown molding, baseboards, and window and door casings. A cabinetmaker is a skilled woodworker who makes furniture.

Built-in furniture can be a great capital improvement for a property. For renters, built-in furniture is obviously not a wise investment, as you can't take it with you in a move.

Designing built-in furniture takes careful planning. Besides the piece itself, the lighting and any necessary electrical outlets must be considered. It's critical to try to anticipate everything when designing built-ins. For example, if you want a telephone jack or internet access at desk level, the wiring will have to be in place before the built-in piece is installed. Details like how far a cabinet door should open are far more easily dealt with while a built-in is still on the drawing board. After the cabinetmaker installs a built-in piece of furniture, it typically needs to be finished, which entails sanding and painting or staining.

An architect or interior designer can design built-in furniture to be constructed and installed by a cabinetmaker. For this, the cabinetmaker uses "shop drawings," which are detailed technical drawings. If you know how to make scale drawings, it's possible to design your own built-in furniture working closely with an experienced cabinetmaker. Since a built-in piece of furniture becomes part of the architecture, make sure that it suits the architectural style of the space. The following are a few options for built-in furniture:

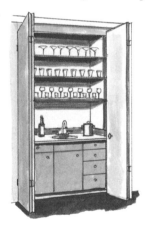

BARS can be built into a living room, dining room, library, or a pantry, to name a few spaces, and are a good idea if you like to entertain. Some older houses have a separate bar area, or sometimes even a separate bar room, with built-in cabinets. When renovating, a bar can be recessed into a wall much like a built-in closet, or built out from the wall like a cabinet, either with or without doors. Ideally, it should include a sink in the countertop, with storage for bottles and supplies below. An icemaker is also convenient, but like a sink it will require a water line, as well as an electrical outlet. Over the countertop, there should be shelves for glasses.

A bar with a sink and running water is known as a wet bar. The countertop can be wood or stone, or any material that is water resistant. Zinc is a classic material for a bar surface, and is common in old French bistros. However, it requires regular maintenance to keep its color and is expensive. Copper is another option and has a country look. The interior of the bar area can be painted a vivid color as an accent, and a mirror can be installed on the wall behind the shelves for glasses to create a glamorous note.

BOOKCASES used to be installed in only the fanciest of houses, because books were a luxury item. As printing technology and literacy rates improved during the seventeenth, eighteenth, and nineteenth centuries, books and book-cases became more commonplace in houses. An open bookcase showing the colorful spines of books adds warmth to a room. In any room where there's open wall space—whether it's a library, office, dining room, or living room—they should be considered for both storage and design purposes.

Some bookcases have open shelves above a lower section with shelves behind doors. The storage space below is great for board games, old photo albums, or other items that you don't want in plain sight. Alternatively, a bookcase may be designed to cover just the lower third of a wall and leave a surface for displaying books and decorative objects at table level. A built-in bookcase may extend all the way to the ceiling, or can stop a foot or two short of the ceiling to allow for decorative objects to be placed on top. It's a cleaner look to have the shelves go all the way to the ceiling. Often, crown molding, which is placed at the transition from the wall to the ceiling, will be continued across the top of a built-in bookcase to help make it appear to be part of the building.

Lighting for bookcases is another important consideration. Lighting may be provided by fixtures recessed into the ceiling, or it may be provided by track lighting. Display light fixtures can be installed into or onto the shelves.

A shelf in a bookcase should be a minimum of 7 to 8 inches deep. Larger books, which can be 11 or more inches deep, can be stacked horizontally but will still require deeper shelves. Consider the books you have to display when designing any new built-in bookcases and be sure the shelves are adjustable so that you can move them up and down. The shelves are more interesting visually when decorative objects are placed among the books. Whether you have bronze bookends, brass bowls, wood boxes, nineteenth-century glass wig stands, a laughing Buddha, or antique opium pipes—bookcases are a great opportunity to display objects that catch your eye.

A **SINGLE HIGH BOOKSHELF** can be an excellent way to create storage in tight spaces. A shelf is installed about 1 foot below the ceiling, ideally around three sides of an alcove or else along one or two walls in a room. This works best when there is no crown molding but rather a clean seam between ceiling and wall. The bookshelf will make the space feel cozy, and books and objects on the shelf will add a splash of color. This type of shelf could also work wonders in a small bathroom that lacks storage for towels and supplies.

HOME OFFICES have become increasingly popular in recent years. Not only are more people working at home, but it's also become standard practice to have personal computers, printers, and other equipment at home as an entertainment and information resource. In a multiuse room, a home office can have doors that conceal a desktop and shelves when they are not in use. The main components of a built-in home office are: a desktop, filing drawers, a pencil drawer (about 4 inches deep) under the desktop surface, bookshelves above or surrounding the desktop, and storage overhead, as well as telephone, electrical, and internet outlets. The typical desk height is 29 to 30 inches, and it's important to make sure there is enough legroom under the desk for comfort. The kneehole—the space for your legs under the desk—should be at least 24 inches high by 24 inches wide to be comfortable. If you have long legs, double-check the clearance you need under the desktop. If you already have a favorite desk chair, then measure the ideal desk height for it.

Drawers can make a built-in office more expensive. Instead of built-in file drawers, it's possible to leave space for a store-bought filing cabinet to slip under the desktop. And a pencil drawer is handy, but not necessary.

Telephone jacks, electrical outlets, and internet cables will be either at desk level or else wires will have to extend down through an opening in the desktop to the baseboard level. If possible, have an electrician raise the outlets to desk level; this typically means opening the wall and then repairing it as needed before installing the built-in desk. If a monitor has to be connected to a computer at floor level, you will need an opening in the desktop for those wires anyway. Consider all the equipment you have—or may want—and ensure there is enough space for everything on the desktop or adjacent shelves.

If the room has a baseboard, it should be continued along the wall behind the desk; this will integrate the desk into the room. A painted wood desktop will need a piece of ¼-inch-thick glass cut to protect the surface. A laminate, such as Formica, can also be used for a desktop.

INGLENOOKS are built-in benches by a fireplace that make for a cozy seating area. They were particularly popular during the Arts and Crafts movement of the second half of the nineteenth century in

DOOR AND DRAWER DETAILS

Kitchen cabinets can have doors and drawer faces with space between them so that the frame of the cabinet is visible, as shown on the left.

Or for a cleaner, more modern look, the doors and drawers may cover the entire front surface of the cabinets, as shown on the right.

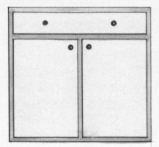 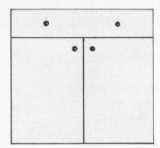

England. The architecture firm McKim, Mead, & White, famous for its designs in the Shingle style, also created built-in nooks. You could

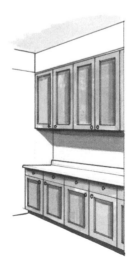

expand on the idea of an inglenook and have built-in benches installed in an underused corner. For an awkward spot in a house, an inglenook or a variation could be a good solution. The seats of such benches can be hinged so that they lift up to allow for storage inside.

KITCHEN CABINETS come in so many styles, the choice can be overwhelming. Start by clipping pictures of kitchens from magazines that catch your eye. Take note of the cabinet details that you like—are the doors flat or paneled, or do they have panes of glass? Think about whether you prefer finishes that are stained wood, painted wood, stainless steel, etched glass, or laminated. Do you like cabinets with crown molding and elaborate details, or favor a simple design? Do you prefer to have the hinges concealed or visible? Keep in mind that traditional-looking cabinets have more details and ornamentation, while modern styles contain fewer decorative elements. It is much easier to begin your search knowing what details you prefer and what look you're after.

Built-in kitchen cabinets are a relatively new phenomenon. A typical Victorian kitchen at the end of the nineteenth century would have had a freestanding cupboard or Welsh dresser to hold dishes and glasses. The cabinets we've come to expect in kitchens today are an innovation of the twentieth century.

The upper kitchen cabinets, known as wall cabinets, may extend up to the ceiling or stop below it. If they stop below, a **SOFFIT** is often created (as pictured on p. 58); it fills the space between the top of the cabinet and the ceiling. The soffit often conceals ducting and pipes. Cabinets that go all the way to the ceiling provide more storage space. Typically, the upper cabinets are 12 or 13 inches deep and the lower ones are 24 inches deep. The bottom of the wall cabinets should be approximately 17 to 20 inches above the countertop.

OPEN SHELVES are less expensive to build than cabinets with doors. Besides being economical, the colors and patterns of the spines of books, china, pottery, or whatever you choose to display will add warmth and coziness to a kitchen—or to any room. The shelves can be long and used in place of kitchen cabinets, or they can be constructed essentially as kitchen cabinets without doors.

FINISHES FOR KITCHEN CABINETS come in a nearly endless variety, which is why you should decide what you like before you start shopping. The finish does much to determine the price of the cabinets, so that might narrow the options. Maple, cherry, hickory, pine, and oak are some wood finishes for kitchen cabinets, and they can all be stained different colors. Rustic-looking wood will show more knots and imperfections than other selections. Thermofoil is the name for a laminate often used on kitchen cabinets as an alternative to natural wood; unlike other laminates, it can be applied over paneled surfaces. Wood kitchen cabinets are usually made with a veneer because solid wood will contract and expand more than a veneer of wood over particle board, for example.

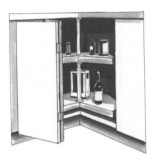

A **LAZY SUSAN CABINET** has a revolving shelf (or two or three) that can be spun around to access items stored at the back of the cabinet. This type of cabinet is typically installed into a corner to provide easier to reach storage. The origin of the term "lazy Susan" isn't known, but it first surfaced in the early twentieth century.

MEDIA CABINETS hold a television, cable box, DVD player, stereo system, or anything else related to watching television or movies or listening to music. Many people like to have a media cabinet with doors, so that when the television is turned off, it's also out of sight. A media cabinet takes careful planning, because the necessary electrical outlets, cable access, and any built-in wiring have to be prepared before the cabinet is installed. The television should be selected before the cabinet design is finalized to ensure there is enough space for the model. Shelves allow a television to be pulled out and swiveled for optimal viewing. A flat screen television can also be mounted to the back of the cabinet on an arm that stretches out and swivels. Before deciding where to place a media cabinet, have a finished furniture plan and confirm that it will be easy to view the television from the sofa and chairs. Also, some are armoires that can be designed to function as media cabinets.

RADIATOR COVERS or ENCLO-SURES hide an unsightly radiator or through-wall air conditioner. Where possible, concealing radiators with a cover is recommended; the covers can be custom-made by a carpenter or bought ready-made. It must have a grille at the top or the front to allow air to flow through, and an access panel to the controls for the heating or cooling unit. There should be a way to easily remove the radiator cover for maintenance. Lattice, which is a framework of crisscrossed wood strips, works well for radiator covers. A radiator cover can be painted the wall color to blend in or with the trim.

WINDOW SEATS use every inch of space in an otherwise awkward area. With bay windows, which project from the face of an exterior wall to create an alcove on the interior, a window seat is an excellent solution for the space. In a tight area, a window seat can be built so that a dining table can be pulled up to it. The top of the seat can be hinged, so that it can be lifted and items stored inside. The seat may be upholstered or have a painted or stained frame with a loose cushion on top. A few added throw pillows make reclining against the wall or windowsill more comfortable. A banquette is a similar type of useful built-in bench but is not located by a window.

Cabinetwork details are what give built-in furniture, free-standing furniture, and architectural woodwork like doors and wall paneling their look. The molding and door style help determine whether a piece of furniture or woodwork has a modern or a traditional appearance.

CABINET DOORS vary greatly in style, from utilitarian kitchen cabinets to beautifully carved antiques. The detailing on cabinet doors does much to determine the overall look of a space.

GLASS-PANED DOORS have either one pane of glass or multiple panes. With multiple panes, there will be strips of wood, called muntin bars, between them, and it looks best when the shelves in the cabinet are lined up with the muntin bars, so that the lines of shelves and panes don't compete. Of course, having a single pane of glass in a door eliminates this problem. In a kitchen, mixing glass-paned and solid cabinet doors can look quite attractive; food and less organized items can be stored behind the solid doors, while plates and glasses can be showcased behind the glass ones. If you opt for this, keep in mind that it's handy to have the cabinets with the dishes near the dishwasher.

PANELING does much to give cabinet doors their character. The panel is a flat plane surrounded by molding. Wood paneling may be used to cover the walls of entire rooms, or just the lower half of the walls. This wall treatment is seen in all architectural styles. The most common place to see panels, however, is on doors—either cabinet doors or full-sized passage doors.

Applied moldings are a way to create the look of a panel by affixing molding to a door, or wall, in a square or rectangle. This adds detail and defines the space. If you have wood doors that are flush, or flat, and would like to add some interest, you can add applied molding and then refinish the door. In a big room, it can help to define the space by

APPLIED   FLAT DOOR   RAISED PANEL   RECESSED
MOLDING   FLAT PANEL

creating square or rectangular panels on the walls with applied molding. Thought must be put into matching the size and proportion of the molding on the wall and the rest of the room. If a mural is painted on a wall, a molding around it can act as a frame.

Flat doors, also called *flush-face doors*, have no paneling or ornamentation. These are the most minimal, with the cleanest lines, and suit a Modern look. However, flat doors might also be found in a country cottage when the look is pared down and simple.

Raised panels are contoured so that the panel has a raised plane. This classic decorative feature is more elaborate and formal than a recessed flat panel. The raised panel can have straight lines or be curved. In European styles, raised panels often have a curved line along the top of the panel.

Recessed flat panels have a panel area that is flat instead of raised, giving it a simple, informal look. It is sometimes called a *Shaker panel*, after the designs of the ascetic Shaker religious sect. Recessed flat paneled doors are often used for kitchen cabinets; they work well with many different looks.

GROMMETS are a covering around an opening. For example, if there's a hole in a desktop that allows wires to reach outlets or a computer below, there will typically be a plastic grommet around the opening. Grommets are used to finish the holes in a cabinet that pin supports are pushed into to support a shelf. You might also find them around the openings along the top of a shower curtain. Grommets give a more finished look, whether to a cabinet, desktop, or shower curtain.

HARDWARE includes all the knobs, hinges, latches, pulls, and slides that allow cabinet doors and drawers to open, close, and be secured. The look of the hardware—or the fact that it is concealed—has much to do with the overall look of the piece of furniture. Scale should be kept in mind when selecting cabinet hardware. For smaller doors, drawers, and cabinets, choose smaller-scale hardware, and the same goes for larger pieces; a tiny cabinet knob won't look right on a substantial cabinet door. Hardware comes in a wide variety of finishes and should be consistent throughout the piece and, as much as possible, with the hardware finish used in the room on doorknobs and such. A stainless steel or nickel finish on hardware with clean lines provides a contemporary look, while hammered iron pulls are more suitable in an Arts and Crafts–style house. Hinges are also quite varied; some are visible from the outside, while others are concealed for a streamlined look.

BALL CATCHES secure a door using one piece that fits into another when the door is closed. Latches such as this and magnetic latches are options when there isn't a proper doorknob to keep the door closed. Even on a passage door between rooms that has a dummy pull (a stationary doorknob), a latch on the doorframe is required to keep the door closed. In general, ball catches are less conspicuous than magnetic catches.

CABINET KNOBS are used to pull open a cabinet door or a drawer. Each knob is secured to the face of a door or drawer at a single point. They can be plain or ornate. Cabinet knobs are generally smaller than cabinet pulls (see below). The choice between the two is a matter of preference, although people who have arthritis or mobility problems in their hands will find a cabinet pull easier to grasp than a knob.

CABINET PULLS typically attach to the face of a door or drawer in two places to create a bar that can be grabbed on to. Cabinet pulls are better than knobs for those who have trouble using their hands. The following are a couple of favorite styles for cabinet pulls:

Bin pulls have an enclosed area to grab on to. They have a distinctive look and are often used for kitchen drawers. Their vintage Victorian style is well suited for anything from a cottage kitchen to a city apartment. Bin pulls are often paired with cupboard catches on cabinet doors (see below).

Edge pulls have a slim curved piece of metal secured to the inside width of a door or a drawer that sticks out just far enough to grasp. Edge pulls are barely visible and are suitable for a clean, contemporary look. They are ideal for use with concealed doors, which are finished the same way as the wall and meant to look like there is no door at all. Edge pulls might be found on drawers and doors in a built-in home office, doors that cover the lower section of a bookcase, or a medicine cabinet.

CUPBOARD CATCHES are mounted on the outside of a cabinet door; a small knob is turned to unlatch the catch and open the door. They are typically used along with bin pulls (see above). Cupboard catches are ideal for use in a butler's pantry or any kitchen with an old-fashioned flair.

DRAWER SLIDES or **DRAWER GLIDES** are tracks that make a drawer (or a shelf) slide smoothly. For use with a shelf, the device may be called a shelf slide or glide. It's a good idea to have drawers on slides, otherwise the side of a drawer might rub against the frame, causing friction and making it difficult to pull the drawer out. Shelves under kitchen counters—or any low shelf, for that matter—should also be put on slides so that they can be pulled out easily to access what is at the back of the shelf. Some slides pull all the way out, while others come out just three-quarters of the way; slides that pull out completely are preferred where possible. Ball-bearing slides are smoother than some plastic slides.

FINGER CUTOUTS, or **FINGER GRIPS,** are the spaces cut into a drawer that allow you to grab onto the face of the drawer to pull it open. This is a simple solution that requires no hardware for opening or closing a drawer. A drawback is it's more likely that fingerprints will show on the surface, but with a slightly glossy paint or with stained wood, this should be relatively easy to clean off. If there's no space for hardware to protrude from the face of a drawer, then this is a viable option. Also, a finger cutout saves the expense of buying hardware.

CANTILEVER

A cantilever is an element that projects horizontally from a wall, without any visible support. Instead, its support is a heavy load at the concealed end, within the wall or otherwise out of view. Cantilevers are used in constructing bridges and buildings. In a house, you might see a cantilevered shelf.

MAGNETIC CATCHES are used to keep a cabinet door closed. The catch has two pieces, one a magnet and the other a metal plate. One piece is fastened to the cabinet frame and the second is attached to the door. Kitchen cabinets (or any cabinet door) can be secured with a magnetic catch—which is a good idea, as a door that doesn't stay closed is bound to drive you crazy.

PIN SUPPORTS are the little metal or plastic pieces that are pushed into openings in the case or outer frame of a cabinet to support a shelf. This is a common way for shelves to be supported in a cabinet or bookcase. Pin supports can be moved up and down to adjust the height of the shelves. When painting a cabinet that uses pin supports to hold up the shelves, be careful not to fill the openings with paint, and be sure to remove the shelves and paint them separately from the case so that they don't get stuck. Grommets, which are coverings around openings, can be combined with pin supports for a more finished look.

SHELF STANDARDS are paired with brackets as supports for shelves; they run vertically on a wall or the inside of a cabinet or bookcase. Shelf standards can be metal or wood. In a utilitarian space, such as a laundry room or a utility closet, metal shelf standards and brackets are an economical way to provide extra storage.

TOUCH LATCHES are operated by tapping on the door and then releasing it. They are used when no hardware is desired on the door. A flat door, with no panels or ornamentation and operated using a touch latch, is a very clean and contemporary look. A barely visible edge pull, in which a slim curved piece of metal is secured to the inside of the door, is an alternative to a touch latch.

JOINTS are created when two or more pieces of material, such as wood, are set together. In cabinetmaking, there are many types of joints, some stronger than others, and some more decorative than others. A few types of joints include the following:

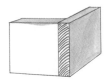 **BUTT JOINTS** are very basic, with two pieces of wood set side by side and no interlocking pieces. The widths of the planks that are touching make up the butt joint. This joint has no strength and needs to be reinforced with glue and dowels, which are plugs of wood inserted into holes drilled into the cross section.

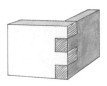 **BOX JOINTS,** also called **FINGER JOINTS,** have interlocking pieces that create a moderately strong joint similar to, but not as strong as, a dovetail joint (as pictured below). The difference between box and dovetail joints is that the interlocking pieces on a dovetail joint are angled to better hold the pieces together. A box joint is easier to make and therefore less expensive than a dovetail; even on some finer antiques, you might find decorative dovetail joints at the front, because they are seen when the drawer is pulled open, but box joints at the back, where the joints are not visible unless the drawer is pulled out completely.

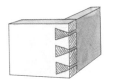 **DOVETAIL JOINTS** are the Rolls-Royces of cabinetmaking joints, being both decorative and also extremely strong. They are made with two interlocking pieces of wood. One piece has a series of flared tenons, or projecting pieces of wood, which fit into a series of mortises, or cavities. Dovetail joints are seen in the finest cabinetwork. Well-known cabinetmakers such as Thomas Chippendale (1718–1779) used dovetail joints when building furniture. This is a dry joint, meaning it isn't bonded with glue.

Dovetail joints are found mostly on drawers and similar boxlike con-
structions, although today they are rarely used in cabinetwork because
they are time-consuming, and thus expensive, to make. Like many
old-fashioned details, dovetail joints have become a dying art.

Blind dovetail joints, also called *lap dovetail joints*,
conceal the joint by leaving about ¼-inch, or
thinner, of solid wood on a drawer front instead
of having the joint cut all the way through the
wood. This type of joint is rarely seen anymore.
It's extremely time-consuming and therefore prohibitively expensive
to produce. Nowadays, a thin board is typically glued over the face of
the drawer to conceal the joint. However, you might still find an
authentic blind dovetail joint on a beautifully made antique.

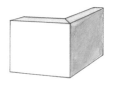

MITER JOINTS (pronounced "mite-er") are
made with two pieces of wood each cut to a 45-
degree angle, so the total joint is 90 degrees.
A miter joint creates a clean edge, where the
seam is barely visible. This type of joint is found
on picture frames and panel end tables, which
have a panel of wood at each end as supports for the tabletop. The joint
is secured by biscuits, which are discs of wood inserted into the cross
section of the boards that touch to make the joint.

MORTISE AND TENON JOINTS consist of a
protruding piece, called the tenon, which fits
into a cavity, or mortise. This is a strong joint
that is common in furniture making; for example, a stretcher on a chair, which connects and
braces the chair legs, might be secured with a
mortise and tenon joint. Antique furniture
often has mortise and tenon joints.

RABBET JOINTS have a piece of wood with a
groove or notch cut into it that fits into another
groove or notch cut into a second piece of wood
(or any material). The word "rabbet" means a
recess cut into the edge or face of a surface.
A rabbet joint might be used in fitting the back panel onto a cabinet,
so that it's flush with the frame, for example.

TONGUE AND GROOVE JOINTS hold two boards together along their lengths. One side has a protruding piece running its length, known as the tongue, and this fits into a groove that runs the length of another board. A V-shaped recess at the joint may add detail. The joint is not glued, which allows for movement, so the boards can expand and contract. For this reason, tongue and groove joints are frequently used for flooring, exterior siding, or wall covering.

The **PROFILE** is the contour of the edge of a shelf, countertop, or tabletop made of wood, stone, brick, or tile. Some profiles, such as ogee and reverse ogee, are more ornate; others, such as a straight edge or a bullnose, have cleaner lines and suit a pared down look. A few commonly used profiles include the following:

BULLNOSE has a half-round edge. This style was popular in the 1970s, when surfaces and edges were rounded, and today can contribute to a retro look.

COVE describes a concave shape with a traditional look. It's more detailed than a straight edge, but not as ornate as an ogee.

OGEE refers to a traditional profile with an S-shaped curve (concave at the top, convex at the bottom). This style has been in use for a long time. An ogee profile creates a traditional and detailed look.

REVERSE OGEE has a convex curve at the top and a concave curve on the bottom—the opposite of an ogee profile.

STRAIGHT EDGE provides a modern look. It may have an **EASED EDGE** (as pictured here), where the top is slightly angled, or beveled, and the rest is a straight vertical line. This is a clean look.

BULLNOSE

COVE

OGEE

REVERSE OGEE

STRAIGHT EDGE

TOE KICKS are the recessed flat baseboards seen on kitchen cabinets, which are usually 4 to 5 inches deep. They serve the practical purpose of allowing space for your toes if you want to stand right up against a counter. A toe kick might also be seen on built-in cabinets; it has a more contemporary look than a traditional baseboard. Like a baseboard, a toe kick also helps to define the area at the base of a piece of furniture, but the term "recessed base" is more likely to be used than "toe kick" when discussing furniture.

Finishing cabinetwork is something to factor into custom-making built-in furniture, and time as well as money should be budgeted for it. If you plan to paint a built-in cabinet, it should be made with paint-grade wood; if the wood is to be stained, then a specific type of wood will be chosen, such as oak or cherry. Much cabinetwork is made with a veneer of wood over some processed wood material. For instance, "cherry cabinets" are typically a veneer of cherry over something else—usually some composite wood product, because it doesn't contract and expand as much as solid wood does. If you opt for solid wood, it might crack as the wood expands and contracts over time. Environmentally friendly composite wood products, such as wheatboard, are available for cabinetwork (see p. 180 for information on wheatboard).

When finishing wood for painting or staining, it is sanded first to ensure a smooth finish, then it is primed and painted or else stained. The inside of drawers and areas that aren't visible on the exterior should be sanded and finished with polyurethane—this will wear better than paint. The molding and built-ins are typically finished with paint that is slightly glossier than the walls, to make them easier to clean; for example, if the wall has flat paint on it, then the molding and cabinets might have paint with an eggshell gloss.

Moldings (spelled mouldings in England) include crown molding, baseboards, and door and window casings. Moldings are often found in traditional or classical styles, less frequently with Modern architecture. When choosing moldings, it's important that their scale suit that of the room. Before ordering crown molding from a catalogue and hoping it works, look at a sample of it tacked up on the wall. There are numerous different types of moldings to choose from, and these include the following:

ASTRAGAL is a symmetrical molding that is used on muntin bars, which separate the panes of a window, or on double doors over the seam between the doors. It's a decorative molding that can have either a simple profile or a more complex contoured one.

BASEBOARDS are installed at the bottom of the wall at floor level. In a traditional setting, the baseboard might be 6 inches high with a contoured profile; in a more streamlined setting, it is more likely to be 4 inches high, with no contouring. With built-ins, such as bookcases, the baseboard should continue over areas of the built-in furniture that are meant to appear to be the wall. For example, a baseboard can be installed at the base of a bookcase, or along the base of a window seat if it is not completely upholstered. This makes the furniture look as though it really is, indeed, built in.

BOLECTION MOLDING is a substantial molding often installed around a fireplace instead of a mantelpiece. When used in place of a mantelpiece, it can be painted the same color as the wall or highlighted in a complementary shade. Installing bolection molding is generally less expensive than buying a mantelpiece.

CHAIR RAILS, also called **DADO CAPS,** are contoured molding installed horizontally around a room approximately 32 inches from

the floor. In the seventeenth and eighteenth centuries in Europe, a chair rail served the practical purpose of protecting the wall from being damaged by the backs of chairs, as it was the style to place them along the walls. Nowadays, a chair rail more typically serves to add interest to a room by dividing the wall. The lower section under the chair rail can be treated differently from the upper section: for instance, the lower section could be painted and the upper section wallpapered. A chair rail is best suited to a room with high ceilings.

CORNER BLOCKS, also called **ROSETTES,** are installed at the corners of door and window casings. They may have a carved bull's-eye or flower motif. Corner blocks make a door or window casing look more finished and so can eliminate the need for curtains on windows. They are often seen in traditional architectural styles.

CROWN MOLDING is installed at the top of the wall to mark the transition between the wall and the ceiling. It can make a ceiling appear to be higher, and can be painted to match either the wall or the ceiling. In England, crown molding is called a cornice.

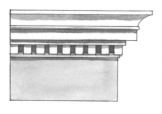

DENTIL MOLDING is a horizontal row of square blocks placed under crown molding to add detail and break up the shadow thrown by the molding above. Dentil molding is best for formal settings, but it is also sometimes seen on kitchen cabinets. The name comes from the French word *dent*, meaning "tooth"—as indeed the molding looks like a row of teeth. This molding was often seen in classical architecture and has a very traditional look.

DOOR OR WINDOW CASINGS, also known as the **ARCHITRAVE,** is molding that frames a door, window, or any opening in a

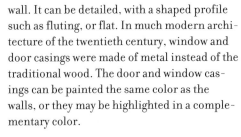

wall. It can be detailed, with a shaped profile such as fluting, or flat. In much modern architecture of the twentieth century, window and door casings were made of metal instead of the traditional wood. The door and window casings can be painted the same color as the walls, or they may be highlighted in a complementary color.

PLINTH BLOCKS are used at baseboard level under a door casing, and sometimes with a window casing. In classical architecture, the plinth is the slab that sits beneath a column or pedestal. Plinth blocks are a detail found in traditional settings and today serve the practical purpose of protecting the door or window casing from damage from things like vacuum cleaners. The plinth block is finished with the baseboard.

SHOE MOLDING is a quarter-round molding that hides the gap between the baseboard and the floor. Such a gap will exist if the floor is not completely even, as is often the case in older houses. If wall-to-wall carpeting is being installed, there should be no need for shoe molding.

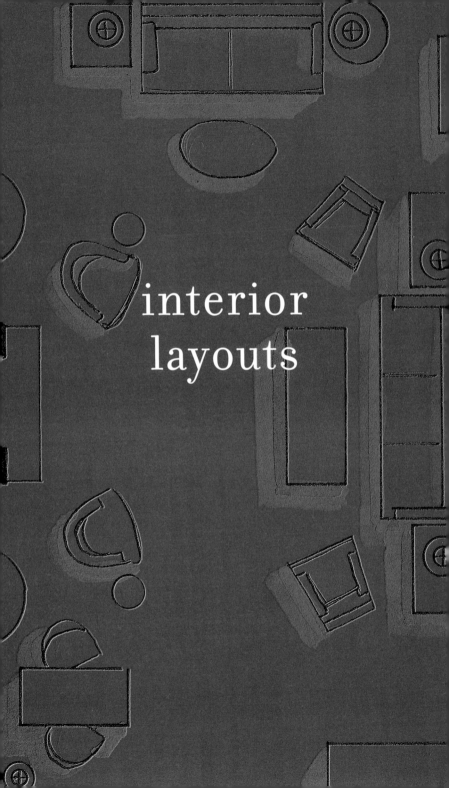

interior
layouts

DURING THE MIDDLE AGES, houses generally had one main room that served as kitchen, living room, dining room, and bedroom. Multiple rooms were only seen in well-to-do households. Over time, the layouts that we are familiar with today developed. It wasn't until the late nineteenth to early twentieth century, for example, that the idea of regular houses having multiple indoor bathrooms surfaced. Since the mid-twentieth century, we've seen an evolution toward an open layout, in which the kitchen, dining, and living rooms are combined in one space. Even more recently, rooms (or areas within rooms) have been designated for uses such as a home office or TV room.

There are two components to space layout: the configuration of the space, meaning where the walls, doors, and windows are located, as well as the room size; and the furniture layout within the space. With both, it is essential to keep in mind the flow, or how the space will be used. Also, the comfort of the people in the space is critical. The lighting and furniture layouts do much to help people utilize a space to its best potential.

While some houses and apartments are truly original in layout, many have *classic layouts* that we see over and over again. Some of these include:

A **CENTER HALL PLAN** is a typical, traditional house layout. In this plan, the front door of the house opens into a central front hall; a staircase to the second floor is located in the front hall. Public rooms, such as the living room and dining room, open into the center hall, as does the kitchen, or a hallway leading to the kitchen. Private rooms are located on the second floor.

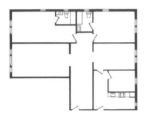

The **CLASSIC SIX** is a traditional layout for an apartment with two bedrooms plus a living room, dining room, kitchen, and a maid's room. It's a term used mainly in New York real estate; around the turn of the twentieth century, the urban middle and upper classes in New York started living in apartments rather than single-family houses as the city grew and many luxury apartment buildings were constructed. Up until this point, apartments in the city were mostly tenements, with minimal amenities and sanitation. The new apartment buildings were designed for a sophisticated market with much more space and grandeur. An apartment with three bedrooms is known as a classic seven, and so on. The term classic six can mean any apartment with six rooms, but it connotes a prewar apartment (built before World War II), which has traditional detailing.

LOFTS are the upper floors of warehouses or industrial buildings, and a converted loft is this space redesigned for residential living. A loft has an open plan with few partitions and lends itself to contemporary decor. In recent decades, the trend in many cities has been to convert commercial buildings into residential lofts, thus changing gritty industrial neighborhoods into upscale destinations. High ceilings, large windows, and minimal architectural details give a loft a sense of openness; however, air ducts and other evidence of mechanical systems are often visible.

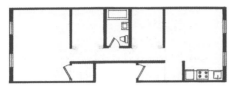

RAILROAD APARTMENTS, also called **RAILROAD FLATS,** consist of a series of rooms in one line, with no hallways dividing them. The rooms are laid out like railroad cars running end to end. This type of apartment was first seen in city tenement build-ings in the early to mid-nineteenth century. This layout involves walking through one room to get to another. A **SHOTGUN HOUSE** is a variation of the railroad apartment often seen in the southern United States.

The *furniture layout* is the placement of furniture in a space. When considering the layout for a room, first think about comfort and the ideal use of the space, and then plan the furniture accordingly. For example, if the room is to be used for entertaining, have comfortable seating for a group.

A furniture plan (as described on p. 37) is used to develop a fur-niture layout before the pieces are moved into or around the room. Making a furniture plan is very helpful when developing furniture lay-outs. If you're trying to configure your old furniture for a new space, for instance, a furniture plan drawn to scale will help you figure out how the pieces will fit. Or if you're shopping for new furniture, a furni-ture plan will tell you what pieces will fit in the space so that you don't waste time considering ones that aren't the right size. Alternatively, using a tape measure and some blue tape, it's possible to mark on the floor the size of the pieces of furniture that you are considering.

Remember as you work on furniture layouts that scale is impor-tant. In a small room, the furnishings and the scale of patterns should be kept smaller, while in a large room, the furnishings and patterns can be bigger. The following are suggestions for furniture layouts:

BEDROOMS should be cozy sanctuaries sheltered from the swirl of daily life. The essential items in a bedroom are: a bed (or two), bed-side tables, and bedside lighting. This room is also typically used for getting dressed and for privacy. For dressing, there should be a chest of drawers with a mirror over it, either freestanding or built-in. Privacy comes with the nature of the room, but a single comfy chair for reading in a corner or by a window can turn the room into an oasis.

If there's space, a *chaise longue* in a corner makes a comfortable spot as well. If you have room for a chair, be sure there's a reading light and an outlet for the light next to it. Today, many bedrooms also have desks. A built-in desk can be very attractive and is a good use of space. A television can be set in an armoire with doors so that it can be concealed when not in use; the armoire should go against the wall opposite the bed and can double as storage if closet space is limited. Alternatively, the TV can be placed on a shelf or on top of a low chest along the wall opposite the bed. For bedside lighting, make sure there are electrical outlets near the bed. A few ideas for bedroom layouts are detailed below:

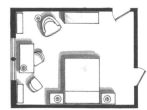

A **FULL-SIZE BED** or a **QUEEN-SIZE BED** should have a bedside table on either side. Avoid pushing a queen-size bed into a corner, as it will be difficult to make the bed and also uncomfortable if there are two people sleeping in it. If space is tight, try at least to have a small aisle between the bed and the wall, as well as a wall-mounted light in the corner. A standard full-size bed is 54 inches wide and 75 to 80 inches long; a queen bed is 60 inches wide by 80 inches long.

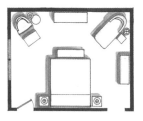

A **KING-SIZE BED** requires a bigger space, but it is roomy and can be more comfortable than other options. Like a queen-size bed, it should have bedside tables on either side. If there isn't room for two bedside tables with a king-size bed, then consider getting a queen instead. If there's space, a narrow bench at the end of the bed can be pretty and offers a place to perch or keep an extra blanket. California kings are beds with a standard size of 72 inches wide by 84 inches long, versus a standard king, which is 78 inches wide by 80 inches long. The box spring for a king-size bed comes in two pieces, so that it can fit through doorways.

Two **TWIN BEDS** in a bedroom is a versatile layout, especially for a guestroom. The beds can be pushed together if desired for a makeshift king-size bed. Moving the beds is easier if the bedside tables are on the outside and there is open space between the beds. In a smaller

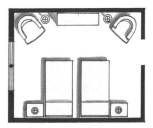

room, it might be necessary to have just one bedside table placed between the two beds. Allow at least 1 foot of space between the beds for bed-making. In a child's room, two twin beds are ideal for sleepovers. Since twin beds are meant for only one person, it's okay to push them up against a wall if space is limited. A wall-mounted light is a space-saving option in tight quarters. A standard twin bed is 39 inches wide by 75 inches long; longer twin beds are available.

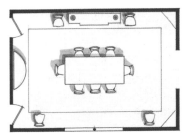

DINING ROOMS usually have a standard layout: a dining table in the center surrounded by dining chairs, and a sideboard along one wall for serving. A corner cabinet, which has a triangular shape to fit snugly into a corner, can be perfect for a dining room; it will fill an empty space and can make the room feel cozy. The dining room is one of the few rooms that doesn't require direct lighting, only background lighting. Typically, there will be a hanging light fixture such as a chandelier over the center of the dining table, and it's best if this has a dimmer, to allow the level of light to be adjusted. Wall sconces wired directly into the wall are common over the sideboard or serving table, and a mirror or painting centered over the sideboard is very suitable. Either built-in or freestanding bookshelves can bring warmth and color to the room. Ideally, there should be 3 feet of open space around the dining table to permit chairs to move in and out easily; this means that the walls, sideboards, or any pieces of furniture should be at least 3 feet from the edge of the table. If you have an area rug under the table, the dining chairs should stand on it fully, not with two legs on and two off. It's a good idea to allow the same 3 feet minimum of space from the edge of the dining table to the edge of an area rug underneath it, meaning that the rug should extend at least 3 feet from the table's edge.

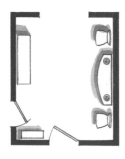

FRONT HALLS, also called **FOYERS,** are located at the entrance to a house and, like a decompression chamber, provide a transition from the outside world to the inside environment. This room typically has a coat closet and an umbrella stand to prepare for the elements when leaving the house or to store outside gear upon returning home. Big, fancy houses traditionally had grand front halls with marble floors and elegant staircases, but even in a modest house a front hall is important for preparing yourself before walking into a central living room. Typically, the stairs in a two-story house ascend from the front hall, so be sure that open doors will not block the bottom of the stairs. If there's space, consider having a bench with a mirror or a painting over it. Alternatively, a console table with a mirror or painting over it and flanked by two side chairs along a wall can work well. It's nice to have a table in a front hall, whether as a place to leave a note or to drop your keys. A chair or a bench is convenient in a front hall to throw a coat on, or as a place to sit down to take off shoes or to wait for someone. In a very large front hall, a central table can be an attractive option.

GREAT ROOMS are large in scale and incorporate the functions of a living room, dining room, TV room, and sometimes kitchen and home office as well. It is a modern trend in architecture.

The kitchen is apt to be at one end of a great room, or close by it. It makes sense to have the dining area next to the kitchen. When planning

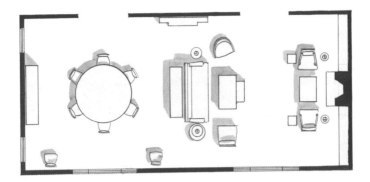

the space, think about where meals will be served from; a sideboard or low table in the dining area can be perfect for this purpose, as well as for storing placemats, silverware, and table accessories such as candlesticks.

If there's a fireplace, the sitting area should be located near it. The sitting area should have a conversation grouping that includes a sofa, an arm chair or two, a coffee table, and a pair of side tables. Make sure there is a place to easily put down a drink by every seat, and at least one place to sit and read with decent lighting. A television can be a part of the seating area, and if so, consider chairs on swivels so that people can turn as necessary to see the screen.

Lighting a great room takes careful thought. Ceiling light fixtures, such as recessed fixtures or track lighting, should be switched to different zones and should have dimmers, so that the lights can be bright in one area and soft in another. A large-scale hanging fixture might also work well. Standing lamps or table lamps will be needed in the center of the room, so make sure there are electrical outlets in the floor for them.

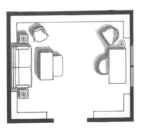

A **LIBRARY** is a traditional room in a house for reading and studying. It comes from the Latin word *librarius* meaning "books." In classical Rome it was fashionable among the wealthy to have one's own library. During the late seventeenth and early eighteenth centuries in Europe, a library with built-in bookcases was increasingly seen in the grandest of houses. The built-in bookcase is still an integral part of a library today, whether its design is contemporary or traditional. Since a library is a room for books, thought should be given to where a person might sit and read in the room. A wing chair is a suitable choice for seating in a library. A small sofa and an upholstered chair with a coffee table in front would also be appropriate. Reading lights are essential, and if the room is to be used during the daytime, take advantage of natural light when possible by placing a reading chair near a window. There will often be a television in a library, though it's quite nice when there isn't. A desk is practical if there's space.

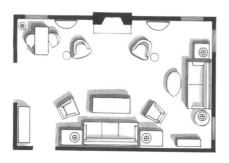

LIVING ROOMS are formal rooms for entertaining, traditionally separate from dining rooms. In France, the living room is called the *salon*, and in England it is known as the drawing room, short for "withdrawing room."

A living room has one or more conversation groupings, depending on its size. A fireplace is a great plus and acts as a focal point for the room. In the same spirit, it's also nice to have a piano in a living room. A grand piano only works in a large room, but a baby grand or an upright piano will fit into a relatively smaller space. The formality of the room is a personal choice. It's possible to have a perfectly functional, kid-friendly living room that works just as well for a party as a simple night at home. It's not practical to have such a precious or formal room that you're nervous about using it.

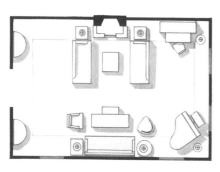

LARGE LIVING ROOMS offer many layout options. One idea—particularly if there's a fireplace in the middle of a long wall—is to have two sofas facing each other on either side of the fireplace, perpendicular to the wall. The two sofas will provide ample seating, and if there's space, another seating area can be added. A pair of console tables on either side of a doorway or a window is also an attractive arrangement. Mirrors or paintings can be hung over the console tables.

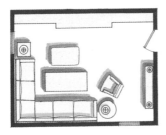

MEDIA ROOMS can range from elaborate state-of-the-art screening rooms to a basic TV room. The placement of the television (or movie screen) is the main consideration. There needs to be room for seating across from it, and a busy doorway should not fall between the television and seating area. The room should be wired for cable and will need electrical outlets near the television. Storage space for the DVD player, DVDs, cable box, and other equipment is also a good idea; this equipment can go into a cabinet, or if there is a flat screen on the wall, in a cabinet or shelf near it.

L-shaped banquettes can provide comfortable seating for many people. Otherwise, a sofa and one or two upholstered chairs work well, too. It's nice to have a coffee table and side tables if there is space.

STUDIO APARTMENTS have one room including a kitchenette, with a separate bathroom. An **ALCOVE STUDIO APARTMENT** has a small area removed from the central area that is just large enough for a bed. Studio apartments are a challenge to decorate, as every inch of space counts; multiuse furniture makes the most of the space. The bare necessities include a bed, a dining table and chairs, a chest of drawers to store clothes, and a comfy chair or two for reading or entertaining. Try to lay out the furniture so that the dining and sitting areas remain separate.

In a particularly small studio, consider a bed that also serves as a sofa, such as a futon, a sofa bed, or a daybed (as pictured here). The downside to these options is that you have to pull out and put away the bed each day. A Murphy bed, which is stored vertically when not in use, is an excellent way to free up floor space—though it doesn't provide seating. A dining table can double as a desk, if need be; in this case, it's practical to have a filing cabinet nearby to keep papers organized. A filing cabinet might also serve as a bedside table in a pinch, or as a side table to a small upholstered chair or sofa. A bookcase doesn't take up much space and helps to keep things uncluttered.

One that is tall rather than wide will take up less floor space. Small spaces get messy fast, so care should be taken to create as much storage space as possible. Putting hooks on the back of doors and adding shelves high on walls can help to accomplish this.

The *kitchen layout* does much to determine how well the kitchen works. That said, the kitchen layout is inherited with a house, and there is little way to change it aside from remodeling. Plumbing lines and electrical outlets are set in place, and moving them requires quite a bit of work.

For a cosmetic change in a kitchen, however, replacing appliances and even a countertop or backsplash is not a major renovation and can do much to improve the look of the room. Changing a vinyl floor in a kitchen is also relatively easy, whereas changing a stone or tile floor requires considerably more work.

If a kitchen lacks countertop space, a quick fix is to get a small table that is 36 inches high, the standard height for countertops. Aisles between a kitchen island and a facing counter, or between two counters, should be at least 42 to 48 inches wide. Some specific kitchen layouts and features are described below:

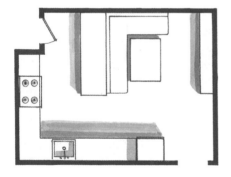

EAT-IN KITCHENS, or **EIKs,** as seen in real estate listings, provide a dining area in the kitchen. An eat-in kitchen will require a table and chairs; a built-in banquette along a wall or one side of a peninsula, which is a counter that runs perpendicular to the wall, is also an option. Lighting is important to consider for an eat-in kitchen. Typically, there is a hanging ceiling fixture such as a lantern over the dining table, recessed fixtures, or track lighting. It's best if the lights over the table can be controlled separately from the other lighting in the room, to provide more control in setting ambience during dinner. Ideally, there will be a cabinet or drawers near the table for storing table accessories such as placemats and flatware.

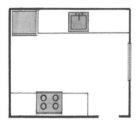

GALLEY KITCHENS are named after the kitchens on boats that, due to space constraints, had to be long and narrow. A galley kitchen has a single straight counter or an aisle between two parallel counters built against the walls. In a kitchen that's tight on space, consider an under-counter refrigerator to maximize counter space. Installing appliances such as microwaves onto the underside of cabinets also frees up countertops.

KITCHENETTES are mini kitchens for a studio apartment, guesthouse, hotel room, or similar tight space. A kitchenette usually runs along a wall in a larger room that is used for other purposes. It can either be open to the room or have doors to conceal it. Complete one-piece units are available with a sink, small refrigerator, cook-top, and oven. Some units have cabinets over the countertop, and others do not. A kitchenette can also be custom-made to exactly fit a space. Both custom-made and prefabricated units require electrical outlets, a water supply, and drainpipes, as well as a gas line if the cooktop or oven is gas. For lighting, under-cabinet fixtures are useful, and a ceiling light from a recessed fixture or track lighting can illuminate the workspace.

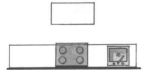

KITCHEN ISLANDS are freestanding cabinets covered with a countertop. They are often used as a dividing element in an open-plan kitchen, which shares the same space with the living and dining areas. The kitchen island became popular in the mid-twentieth century during the Modern movement. An island can have a cooktop or sink. If there is a cooktop, ventilation must be considered. Kitchen islands can be the standard countertop height, 36 inches high, or may be elevated to 42 inches high for bar-stool seating. When two or three bar stools are pulled up to an island, it makes cooking for a group a much more social project.

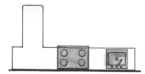

KITCHEN PENINSULAS are countertops with cabinets below that extend
out from a wall perpendicularly. It is similar to a kitchen island, the difference
being that an island stands on its own. In
geology a peninsula is a spit of land that projects from the mainland;
Cape Cod and most of the state of Florida are peninsulas. The word
peninsula comes from the Latin *paene* meaning "almost" and *insula*
meaning "island." In an open kitchen-living room, a peninsula is a
good way to divide the space. In a small-scale eat-in kitchen, where
every inch counts, a built-in banquette might be installed along the
outside of a peninsula for seating at the dining table. Bar stools can
also provide additional seating around a peninsula.

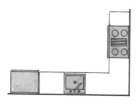

L-SHAPED KITCHENS have two
counters that meet in a right angle like the
letter "L." In this layout, a breakfast table
often fits in the open space opposite the
counters. Keeping the work triangle in
mind (see p. 87), it's best not to put the
sink, refrigerator, and stove in a row along the same counter. One of the
three should be on the opposite countertop across from the other two.

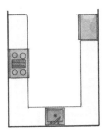

U-SHAPED KITCHENS have three straight countertops that form a "U." Preferably, the sink is in the center with a window above, the refrigerator off to one side, and the cooktop or range on the other side. This layout lends itself to a kitchen island, which can go across the open end if the room extends to a living or dining area. A peninsula also creates more counter and storage space.

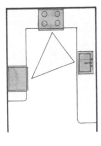

The **WORK TRIANGLE** is the much discussed relationship between the three main centers of activity in the kitchen: the refrigerator, the sink, and the stovetop. When a person is cooking, he is constantly moving between these three areas. No matter where you put these items—unless they are in a straight line—they will form a triangle. Keep in mind that they should be a comfortable distance from each other—a few steps away.

Staircases serve the practical purpose of allowing you to get from one level of a house to another. Their design is dictated by the available space. The **RISER** is the vertical part of the step, and the **TREAD** is the horizontal part on which you step. Ideally, the riser is no higher than 7 ½ inches and no lower than 6 inches, and the tread should be between 10 to 12 inches deep. The **NOSING** is the edge that projects from the tread. A **FLIGHT** refers to an uninterrupted series of steps running between floors or landings.

Building codes will have much to say about a staircase. The slope, or steepness, of it, the height of the handrail, and the minimum size of a landing, for example, are issues the building code will weigh in on. Double-check on plans for a new staircase to make sure that no one will bump his or her head on the ceiling when walking down the stairs. There are many designs and details for a staircase; a few basic ones are as follows:

CLOSED-STRING STAIRS have a board, called the string, which does not follow the line of the treads and risers, meaning that it's visible above the steps. This board runs along the edge of the stairs and

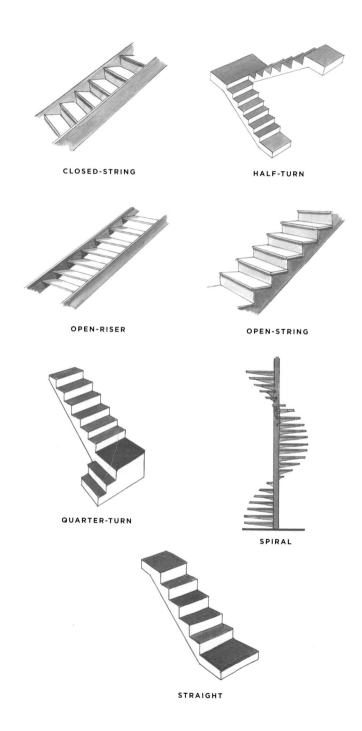

CLOSED-STRING

HALF-TURN

OPEN-RISER

OPEN-STRING

QUARTER-TURN

SPIRAL

STRAIGHT

slopes at the same angle. In England, most staircases were closed string until the early eighteenth century, after which the open-string style became more popular.

HALF-TURN STAIRS turn 180 degrees at the landing. If there is an open space between the flights, it has an "open well." If there's space on the landing, it's quite nice to have a narrow bench for resting mid-climb.

OPEN-RISER STAIRS have no risers, which are the vertical elements in a step. Instead, there is open space between the treads. This type of stair has a modern look.

OPEN-STRING STAIRS have a board that slopes at the same angle as the stairs, called the string, which is cut to follow the line of the steps so that it doesn't extend above the steps. The balusters, which are the supports for the handrail, connect directly to the treads.

QUARTER-TURN STAIRS are probably the most typical layout for a staircase in a house. They have a right-angle turn with either a landing or a few **WINDERS,** which are wedge-shaped steps, to make the turn.

SPIRAL STAIRS are constructed around a central newel post and have wedge-shaped steps. Spiral staircases can either be freestanding or surrounded by a wall, as in older architecture where a staircase was set into a tower. A spiral staircase is best used when space is constricted; they are quite difficult to go up and down. In a traditional library, it is typical to have a spiral stair going up to a balcony where another level of books is shelved.

STRAIGHT STAIRS are a straight flight without any landings or changes in direction. It's nicer to have a turn on a staircase, but when there's no room, a straight staircase does the trick.

Storage space is critical for a house to function properly. If you can't find anything, or stuff falls out onto your head every time you open a closet door, you won't be very happy in your house. If you are building, renovating, or just sprucing up, think about where you will store your vacuum cleaner, mops, brooms, and cleaning supplies.

LONG-TERM STORAGE

As much as you try to avoid it, sometimes putting belongings into storage is the only option if you want to hang on to family antiques or extra pieces of furniture. Valuable items, especially prints, papers, and paintings, should not be stored in the basement, which is prone to flooding and mold. Long-term storage elsewhere is a better option if there is no other space for them.

Take photographs of each item to be put into storage and make a list of them with detailed descriptions and measurements. This will prove valuable if you're moving and want to work on a furniture plan for the next house. Instead of having to go into the storage space to look at what you have, you can just refer to your list and photographs and create a furniture plan from them. This is also an excellent idea for insurance purposes.

Where will you put linens, tools, card tables, folding chairs, skis, ice skates, and badminton equipment? Will there be a home for the DVD player, TV, CDs, speakers, photo albums, the chess set, sun hats, dirty laundry, clean sheets, muddy shoes, pots and pans, the iron and ironing board, old bank statements, and suitcases? If everything has its place, the house will be organized and tidy.

CLOTHES CLOSETS should be 25 to 30 inches deep and have a clothes pole that is at least 3 to 4 feet long. The height of a single clothes pole is typically about 60 to 66 inches, though taller people may want it to be higher. When moving or renovating, or simply changing a closet, measure the length of the hanging space you currently have and from there determine how much space would be ideal. It's possible to double hang clothes poles, so that one is above another; carefully measure the length of pants, shirts, and jackets to determine the correct heights of the poles. Make sure you can easily reach the top pole. A walk-in closet may range from 5 to 15 feet deep or more, and has clothes poles running along one or all of the walls.

The **FRONT HALL CLOSET** should be near the front door in the entryway. It should have a pole for hanging coats and solid wood hangers—a front hall closet is no place for flimsy wire hangers. One smart design has a shelf or two over the pole, which provides a place to put hats or bags. Where possible, have the closet light wired so that it turns on and off as the door is opened and closed; this is called a jamb switch and requires some electrical work to install. If the budget allows, it can be stylish to wallpaper the inside of a front hall closet. Unlike other closets, this one is quite public, and wallpaper can be a chic surprise. The wallpaper or paint color for the closet doesn't have to match the walls in the foyer—it's almost better as its own little statement. A few hooks should be mounted on the walls in the closet.

LARDERS are small rooms for storing food. A larder provides convenient storage for dry, canned, and paper goods; in Spain, for example, you might find a large ham hanging from a hook attached to the ceiling in a larder. U-shaped or L-shaped shelves may provide storage, with space underneath the shelves for larger items such as a vacuum cleaner or boxes of bulk items.

Previously, the larder was built into the north side of a house, which was known to be the coolest. The location is not as important now that there is refrigeration.

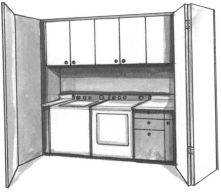

LAUNDRY CLOSETS or **LAUNDRY ROOMS** have a washing machine and dryer and, if there's space, shelves for storing cleaning supplies or even a sink and drying rack. Ideally, there will be a separate laundry room, but this isn't always possible. In this case, a laundry closet is effective; doors conceal it when the machines aren't in use. A washing machine will require water lines, and the dryer will have to be vented; both need electrical outlets as well. To be practical to install, a laundry closet or laundry room should be located near existing water lines and in a place where it won't be too complicated to run a vent.

LINEN CLOSETS in early houses would have been served by a linen press, which is a cabinet with hanging space above and drawers below. A built-in linen closet should have shelves at least 18 inches deep to hold folded sheets and towels. Ample storage space for linens helps to keep items neat and organized. Preferably, there will be enough space to separate the linens by size or function—for instance, one pile for twin-size sheets, and another for king-size. Extra blankets and pillows, a sewing kit, ribbon, and wrapping paper can also be tucked away in a linen closet.

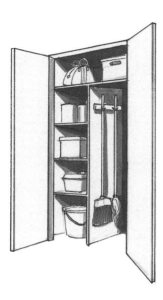

UTILITY CLOSETS are the catchall closets for vacuum cleaners, tool kits, brooms, mops, buckets, feather dusters, extra paper towels, and other bulky items. A utility closet works best with a mix of shelves and some open space to hang mops and brooms, and should be large enough to fit a vacuum cleaner.

kitchens

5

IT USED TO BE that in some middle- and most upper-class houses, the kitchen was the servants' domain and rarely visited by the family of the house. This changed around the mid-twentieth century, as the kitchen increasingly became the heart of the house—a place where family members cook, dine, watch television, and enjoy each other's company. In essence, this was a return to much earlier times, when the kitchen, with its warm fire, was at the center of most indoor activities.

When planning a kitchen, it's easy to get swept up in the excitement of brand names and bells and whistles. In a renovation, first determine what you want from the space before focusing on issues like stainless steel versus granite countertops. How many people typically cook at once? Do you bake pastries? Do your kids like to do their homework in the kitchen? Plan accordingly for such activities. If you want a TV in the kitchen, think about where it will go and from where it will be visible. If you have an open plan, where the kitchen, living, and dining areas are all one space, decide how the kitchen area will function within the overall layout and for entertaining. Finally, decide on the look and begin to cull through the overwhelming number of options for cabinets, appliances, and countertops. Remember that for cooking purposes, it's not the size of the kitchen that matters, but how well it functions. For more information on kitchens, see also page 58 and page 84.

Appliances have literally changed the way we live. Without them, we would spend most of our time trying to keep the household running by maintaining fires in the kitchen, scrubbing clothes and dishes, and hauling ice blocks for refrigeration.

Appliances are also constantly evolving. There are new models on the market all the time with improved technology, combined tasks (such as coffee making and microwaving), and additional extra features. When making your selections, always keep energy efficiency in mind. Some appliances have Energy Star ratings, indicating that they are particularly energy efficient—and meaning that they will save money on bills, as well as wear and tear on the environment. Also think about what you really need: if there are only two people in the house, you probably don't need an enormous family-size refrigerator and freezer. Be sure to check that the house's electrical system can meet the energy requirements of your appliances; some require 240 volts, which might not be available in an older house.

The finish on appliances contributes to the look of the kitchen. Stainless steel has been popular recently and has an industrial and modern look; however, it shows fingerprints, and magnets usually won't stick to it. An **INTEGRATED PANEL** on an appliance such as a dishwasher makes it blend in with the cabinetwork, giving the kitchen a unified look.

Buying an appliance is like buying a car. There are high-end, high-performance, attention-grabbing appliances that have become status symbols; and then there are not-so-flashy, workaday appliances that get the job done. Into that mix, add energy-efficient appliances. Your budget, your priorities, the look of the kitchen, and how much you cook will be considerations in your decision on what to buy. Talking to a knowledgeable salesperson is helpful. What follows is some general information as a starting point; each brand will have variations and different names for its features.

COOKTOPS are set into a countertop for cooking over a direct heat source. They can be electric or gas. A relatively new option is an induction cooktop, which has an electric coil under a ceramic surface; when a pot made with a magnetic-based material, such as steel or iron, is placed on the burner, heat is transferred directly to the pot and the burner doesn't get hot. Induction cooktops aren't just for people who prefer electric, they are a particularly safe and energy efficient because the cooktop doesn't heat up. Gas cooktops have burners measured in Btus, or British thermal units—the amount of heat required to raise the temperature of 1 pound of water by 1 degree. A burner with 15,000 Btus will put out more heat than a burner with 12,000 Btus, and this will affect how fast a pot of water will boil.

A cooktop is typically 30 or 36 inches wide and is used in conjunction with a built-in oven. The alternative to a separate cooktop and built-in oven is a range, which is one unit with both burners and an oven. Some cooktops have a downdraft exhaust fan that pulls fumes into a ventilation system, or you may opt for a venting hood and an exhaust fan above.

The **DISHWASHER** was invented in 1886 in Shelbyville, Illinois, by Josephine Garis Cochran. Her dishwasher, the first usable model, was patented and displayed at the 1893 Chicago World's Fair. Despite early interest from commercial venues like restaurants, it didn't catch on for residential use until the mid-twentieth century.

Usually, the dishwater is placed next to a kitchen sink so that dishes can be rinsed and loaded into the dishwasher in one motion. Reserving the cabinets above a dishwasher for plates and glasses is convenient as well. Some models are louder than others, which is something to consider especially if you have an open layout and will be eating dinner or watching television nearby. Moving or adding a dishwasher entails bringing in a water supply line and a drain, as well as an electrical outlet.

DRYERS draw in air, heat it up, and blow it across clothes that are being bounced around inside a rotating drum. Early clothes dryers were barrels turned by hand over open fires— a much more labor-intensive activity than pressing a button or two.

Dryers run on either gas or electricity. Gas is said to dry clothes with less creasing; it will also keep your electric bill down. Almost all dryers need an exhaust vent. Separate washing machines and dryers can be stacked to conserve space; a "stacking kit" provides the parts necessary to support the dryer over the washer. Some units come prestacked with the dryer over the washer. Another possibility is a combination washer and dryer, which handles both processes in one machine. These models have been used in Europe for a long time and are gaining ground in the United States. They are compact, convenient (you don't have to switch clothes from washer to dryer), and can fit under a countertop. Typically, combination washer/dryers don't require a vent for the dryer, which makes installation easier. The downside is that the whole cycle from start to finish takes a long time, and loads have to be relatively small. A stacked washer and dryer, or the combination unit, can make it possible to have a washer and dryer in a small apartment.

Remember that even with a top-notch dryer, there's still the natural drying solution—the clothesline—which is an eco-friendly option whenever the sun is out. A clothesline may not be nice to look at, but between saving energy and the crisp freshness of line-dried sheets and clothes, it's a good alternative to a dryer. For apartment dwellers or during cold weather, drying racks are an option for smaller items.

FREEZERS work on the same principle as refrigerators, removing heat from the inside of an enclosed and insulated space using a vapor compression system. A freezer is usually a component of a refrigerator, although a family might consider a dedicated freezer for storing large items of food; in this case, it can be put in the basement or garage, where it will be out of the way. Freezers come both as upright models, with doors that hinge vertically, and ones that open at the top with a horizontally hinged door.

GARBAGE DISPOSALS grind bits of vegetables, fruit rinds, and similar organic garbage into a pulp before sending it into the sewage system. It cuts down on the volume of garbage thrown out. A disposal is installed under the kitchen sink and opens into the sink drain. From there, the ground-up food enters the sewer system and is treated like any wastewater in the house. One drawback to a garbage disposal is that food left sitting in it can become smelly. An environmentally conscious alternative to a garbage disposal is to compost organic waste and use the end products of composting for fertilizer.

KITCHEN OFFICE

When designing a kitchen, consider including a built-in desk. The kitchen has increasingly become the heart of the house, and a desk there might be an ideal place to pay bills and write notes. A computer can be handy to look up recipes, or to check e-mail while dinner is roasting. If there's room for it, a desk can be a great addition to the kitchen.

ICEMAKERS are extremely useful and are much easier than filling ice trays with water, carrying them to the freezer (without spilling), and then trying to neatly extrude the frozen cubes hours (or days) later. Freezers often have built-in icemakers. However, icemakers are also sold as a separate unit (as pictured here). If you have a separate bar that is not near the kitchen, it is handy to install a small icemaker in it. An icemaker requires a water supply line and an electrical outlet. While the icemakers found inside full-size freezers will meet the requirements of most families, a second one is a great convenience for a large family or people who entertain a lot.

INSTANT HOT WATER DISPENSERS have a spout for near-boiling water. This can be a great timesaver for making tea, instant soup, thawing frozen foods, or for whatever might require very hot water pronto. Instant hot water dispensers have a water tank with an electric heating coil that mounts under the sink, and the spout fits into a precut opening in the sink. An instant hot water dispenser requires a water supply line and an electrical outlet. Some models come with a second spout for filtered cold water as well. If you don't have the opening in your sink for this appliance, consider a countertop hot water heater that plugs in; it also heats water very quickly.

OVENS are enclosed heated chambers used for baking, roasting, broiling, and so forth. American Colonial houses often had baking ovens built into a wall next to a fireplace. The bulging stone wall would hold the heat from the fireplace to warm the oven. Today, ovens are fueled by gas or electricity. If possible, try to have two ovens in a kitchen; it will make cooking large meals much easier. These days, there are microwave ovens, convection ovens, conventional ovens, and steam ovens; each cooks food a different way, as detailed below.

BUILT-IN OVENS are installed into a wall or below a countertop and are often used in conjunction with a separate cooktop unit. This can be done with a conventional oven, microwave oven, steam oven, or convection oven. A double built-in oven has two separately controlled ovens (as pictured here). Wall ovens come in a variety of widths, so make sure the oven you get fits into the available space in the cabinetwork or wall. If the built-in oven is being installed under a countertop, it usually has to be electric. For people with bad backs or who have trouble bending over and lifting up things like heavy roasting pans, a built-in oven installed on the wall will make life easier.

CONVECTION OVENS use a fan to circulate hot air throughout the oven; this causes the food to cook faster and makes the heat more even throughout the oven. Convection ovens can be either gas or electric, and the convection fan can be switched on or off. When the fan is turned off, the oven cooks food just like a conventional oven, in which hot air rises to the top of the oven. One advantage to this type of oven is that hot air blown onto food transfers heat faster, thus cooking the food more quickly at lower temperatures, which is more energy efficient. In addition, many convection ovens automatically adjust the temperature, so if you are following a recipe you can enter the temperature you would use with a conventional oven and the convection oven will translate that into the appropriate temperature. There are two types of convection ovens: "regular convection" and "true convection." The true convection is recommended, as it has a heating coil around the fan to improve the convection action.

MICROWAVE OVENS employ high-frequency electromagnetic waves, called microwaves, to cook food. The food itself heats up, but not the air around it, meaning that food can cook much faster than in a conventional oven. The microwave oven was invented by accident in the mid-1940s. Microwaves were being utilized for radar systems in World War II, and an engineer named Percy Spencer, who worked at Raytheon Company, had a chocolate bar in his pocket as he stood near a device that emitted them; when the chocolate started to melt, he realized that microwaves might also be used to cook food. The first microwave ovens were huge and weighed hundreds of pounds, but by the late 1960s, smaller models had been developed for residential use. Despite the drawbacks of not always heating food evenly and not browning food as in a conventional oven, microwaves have become a standard kitchen item.

There are models designed to be built-in, placed on a countertop, or mounted under cabinets over the countertop, which is a good idea when space is tight. Some have a built-in exhaust fan and can be installed over a cooktop. A microwave requires an electrical outlet.

STEAM OVENS are said to produce healthier food than conventional ovens. By cooking with steam that is piped into the oven compartment, fewer nutrients are lost in the cooking process and less oil and butter need to be used compared with a conventional oven. In addition, food doesn't dry out the way it does in a conventional oven, and the skin of a chicken, for example, actually comes out crispy. One drawback is that food doesn't brown as it does in a conventional oven.

Most steam ovens come with a booklet of recipes, including the obvious steamed vegetables, as well as ideas for roasting chickens, baking brownies and cheesecakes, or poaching fish, among others. A steam oven requires an electrical outlet and either has to be connected to a water line in the wall or have a water tank that needs to be filled. There are also combination convection and steam ovens.

RANGES are single units with a combination of burners on top and one or two ovens below. In the mid- to late nineteenth century, ranges were fueled by coal and made of cast iron. The gas range appeared toward the end of the nineteenth century, and it gained popularity over the next few decades. Electric ranges were also available around the turn of the twentieth century, but they were expensive and didn't become popular until much later. This was partly due to the fact that not everyone had electric service, and partly because the temperature was not as easy to regulate as with gas. Temperature regulation has improved since then, and today both gas and electric are good options. Some say that electric ovens have more consistent temperatures than gas ovens, while others insist that gas is the only way to go.

Today, whether a range runs on gas or electricity, both typically require electrical outlet. A gas range needs the electricity for the pilot light, clocks, timers, and such. Having an electric pilot light on a gas oven, instead of a gas pilot light that's always on, will save on gas. **DUAL-FUEL** ranges combine gas burners with an electric oven, for people who prefer that setup. Ranges can come equipped with one oven or two, a broiler, griddles, extra burners, timers, convection ovens, and more. The key is to decide what you need before you shop, so as not to be overwhelmed by the options. Make sure the width of the range you select fits into the kitchen the way you want. Any type of range will require an exhaust fan.

Aga is a brand of range that is perpetually warm. It has a beautiful, classic design and was invented by the Nobel prize-winning physicist Dr. Gustav Dalén and first patented in 1922. The concept was to invent a range that needed no tending to, and the result was the

Aga—always on at the right temperatures, and needing no dials or switches. The ranges are made out of cast iron and well insulated, so they don't lose much heat, though they will keep a kitchen warm. Aga ranges, which are rather expensive, can use natural or propane gas, oil, or electricity. The original design has been expanded upon and now comes in dual-fuel options, with conventional gas stovetops and electric ovens; these ranges have dials and can be switched off. An Aga works well for a big country house where the winters get chilly. Some chefs swear by their Agas, and others love the bright colors the ranges come in.

The words "stove" and "stovetop" are holdovers from an earlier era. A stove is something that burns fuel, or electricity, to generate heat. Until the nineteenth century, stoves were mainly used for heating rooms. Then a model was developed that had grates for cooking food as well. Cabins and farmhouses often still use a wood-burning stove for heat, and sometimes even for cooking.

REFRIGERATORS typically use a vapor compression refrigeration system to remove heat from inside an insulated box, thereby keeping what's inside cool. For thousands of years, people have been creating cool spaces to preserve food. In ancient times, people living in cold climates had snow cellars, which were dug into the ground and insulated with material such as straw and wood. Blocks of ice, one of the earliest methods for keeping a small space cold, were regularly used up until the early twentieth century. The "icebox" was a precursor to the modern refrigerator, with one compartment for a block of ice and another to store food; the ice melted into a tray, which had to be emptied periodically. In addition, up until the twentieth century houses regularly had larders, which were cool storage rooms for food.

An American physician named John Gorrie built one of the first refrigerators in the mid-nineteenth century. Early models used ammonia as a coolant, but it was toxic and smelled if it leaked. By the 1930s, refrigerators were becoming more common, and E.I. du Pont de Nemours and Company trademarked Freon, a chlorofluorocarbon (CFC) to be used instead of ammonia. Much later, it was determined that chlorofluorocarbons damage the ozone layer, and today, less harmful refrigerants are used.

Refrigerators are measured in cubic feet. One person might need only 8 or 9 cubic feet, while 18 cubic feet might suit a small family, and a large family may require as much as 29. People tend to have smaller refrigerators in the city, as they shop for food more frequently, in small amounts, and have less kitchen space. In the country or the suburbs, refrigerators tend to be bigger, because kitchens have more space, stores are farther away, and people can load up their cars with groceries. Make sure the refrigerator door opens in the right direction for your kitchen layout, and leave about 2 inches of space on the side for it to open. Some refrigerators aren't very deep, so before making a final selection, check that your cookie sheets or favorite roasting pan will fit into it; you can even measure the biggest pots and pans you have that might need to go in the fridge, to see if it will work.

Counter-depth refrigerators are approximately 24 inches deep—the same measurement as most standard countertops. The doors and handles to this fridge usually stick out past the 24-inch mark, so if you're putting it in a tight space, double-check the overall measurement including the doors and handles; this is typically closer to 28 or 29 inches deep.

If a refrigerator has an icemaker or dispenses chilled water, it will require a water supply line. There are a few different styles for a refrigerator:

FRENCH DOOR REFRIGERATORS have two side-by-side refrigerator doors over one freezer drawer below. The top refrigerator section is one compartment; there is no internal divider between the two doors. This design combines the benefit of a side-by-side refrigerator, in which the narrow doors are well-suited to small spaces, with the advantage of having the freezer either over or under the refrigerator, where the compartment is relatively wide—both allow you to store bigger and bulkier items.

REFRIGERATOR DRAWERS can have both a freezer drawer and a refrigerator drawer that fit one over the other into a compact area. In tight quarters like a kitchenette, where only a small refrigerator will work, these are a good option. They also come in handy in a bar area, media room, or a home office. The drawer is pulled out to view the refrigerator contents.

REFRIGERATOR-OVER-FREEZER models have a freezer drawer below and the refrigerator above. The freezer and refrigerator compartments are wider than in a side-by-side refrigerator, so larger items are more easily stored. Since there aren't as many shelves as in a side-by-side model, items are more likely to get stacked on top of

FRENCH DOOR

REFRIGERATOR-
OVER-FREEZER

SIDE-BY-SIDE

TOP FREEZER

UNDER-COUNTER

each other in the freezer. Getting food out of the freezer entails bending and lifting, so if you have back trouble, another model might be better suited for you.

SIDE-BY-SIDE REFRIGERATORS have two doors side by side. This model suits a small space, as the doors require less clearance to swing open than the deeper doors of a model with the freezer built over or under the refrigerator. However, since the fridge and freezers are narrow, it won't be easy to store a large platter or a 27-pound turkey in a side-by-side refrigerator. Most oversize refrigerators (those over 42 inches wide) will have side-by-side doors, as a single wide door would be too heavy; these have bigger compartments, so a roasting pan or big holiday goose should fit.

TOP FREEZERS are the old-fashioned refrigerator design, with the freezer compartment on top. This style is useful if you use the freezer a lot. The lowest shelves or drawers in the refrigerator are down near your feet, and it can be difficult to see what's there. Both the freezer and refrigerator hold relatively large items quite easily.

UNDER-COUNTER REFRIGERATORS fit under countertops, are smaller in proportion, and have doors that hinge vertically. They can be two side-by-side units, one a freezer and the other a refrigerator, or one refrigerator unit with a small freezer in it. In a small kitchen with limited counter space, this can be a very good idea to maximize every inch of the work area. This model is also quite practical for a bar or TV room.

TRASH COMPACTORS squeeze garbage down into a compact form so it's less bulky. This means that you don't have to take the garbage out as often, and it is easier to handle—though a compressed bag of trash can be heavy. One drawback is that garbage left too long in the compactor may begin to smell, though filters are available to ameliorate this. Also, if you have children, get a trash compactor with a safety feature to prevent them from using it, as the compressor packs up to a walloping 5,000 pounds of pressure and will crush anything in it. Compactors are available in both freestanding and under-counter models; the kind you choose depends on where you plan to install it. Trash compactors are found more frequently in rural houses; in the city, garbage tends to be collected more often.

 **VENTING HOODS** are the external elements of a kitchen exhaust system that go over a cooktop or range. The hood and corresponding ventilation system should be compatible with your cooktop or range, and also with the size of the room. Some styles extend out from the wall, while others are designed to hang from the ceiling over a kitchen island. Instead of a hood, some cooktops and ranges have a built-in downdraft exhaust fan, which draws air down from the cooking surface.

WASHING MACHINES came in a variety of early forms. In the late eighteenth and nineteenth centuries, clothes were wrung, slammed, twisted, and dunked by different types of hand-operated machines.

The age-old method of scrubbing clothes on rocks can still be seen today in places such as India where *dhobi wallahs*, or washer men, beat clothes clean on rocks along the banks of rivers and streams. The first electric washing machine was developed in the early twentieth century, and improvements have continued ever since.

Washing machines can be either front loading or top loading. Front-loading machines (as pictured here) have a horizontal axis, so the clothes go up and over an imaginary horizontal bar. They are more energy-efficient than top-loading machines, which have a vertical axis. A front-loading washing machine also has a flat top, which can be handy for folding clothes.

A washing machine requires an electrical outlet, a water supply line, and a drain. When planning a laundry area, also think about the shelving and storage to keep items like detergents organized. A sink is extremely useful in a laundry room; to make room for this in a small space, the washer and dryer can be stacked.

WINE COOLERS provide storage at ideal temperatures for bottles of wine. If there's an oenophile in the house, then a wine cooler makes a perfect addition. Some models fit under the countertop, and others are freestanding; larger ones can store 150 bottles or more. A pantry or bar area is an ideal location for a wine cooler.

Backsplashes are the vertical surfaces above a countertop, typically finished with a material that can be cleaned easily. The backsplash can be as little as 4 inches above the countertop, or it may extend from the countertop to the bottom of the kitchen cabinets, which is neater and requires less maintenance.

The backsplash can be made of the same material as the countertop, or something entirely different. If you have wallpaper in the kitchen and want to continue it on the backsplash, the wallpaper can be protected by a ¼-inch-thick piece of clear glass. Other ideas for backsplash and countertop combinations include: a granite or marble countertop and stainless steel backsplash (or vice versa) for a sophisticated look; a solid synthetic (such as Corian) countertop and white subway tile backsplash for a clean and contemporary look; or a butcher block countertop and tile backsplash for a country look. The possibilities are nearly endless, and browsing through photographs in books and magazines will help to generate ideas. Changing the backsplash can provide an excellent face-lift for a kitchen, if a full renovation is not planned.

Countertops must be water resistant and strong enough to hold up against the cutting, banging, and clunking around of pots, pans, and bowls that happen daily as food is prepared. They are also a significant decorative element in the kitchen and do much to set the tone of the design. Keep in mind that countertops don't have to be all one material. If you have wood countertops, for example, it's a good idea to put stone, glass, or stainless steel around the cooking areas, so that you can set a hot pot directly onto the countertop. Granite and stainless steel can be alternated for a contemporary and sleek look. If you love to bake, an area with a cool marble countertop might be useful for rolling out dough; be sure not to place it near an oven or appliance that produces heat.

Consider how stain resistant a material is. Some stone countertops can be polished to a have a shiny surface, or else honed for a flat finish; honed stone countertops are more likely to stain than polished ones. Other types of stone aren't typically polished. Materials such as solid synthetics and butcher block can be sanded to remove stains whereas laminates such as Formica can't be refinished but are less expensive to replace down the road.

The countertop layout must also be carefully planned. There should be open countertop space next to cooking surfaces and ovens. Consider where the serving surface will be—from counter space on the island, or next to the range along a wall?

The standard counter height is 36 inches, and the standard depth is 24 inches, but you might want to consider something different. The world-famous chef Julia Child (1912–2004) was 6 feet 2 inches tall and had her maple countertops in Cambridge, Massachusetts, built 2 inches higher than standard. For a tall family, higher countertops can make a kitchen more comfortable to work in.

Countertop edges of concrete, stone, wood, and solid synthetic come in a variety of profiles, which are the contours of the edge. Detailed examples of profiles are listed on p. 69.

Cost is a factor in choosing countertops. Laminates generally are the least expensive. The cost of stone and wood varies depending on the specific selection, but both will be more pricey than laminate. Concrete is a relatively expensive choice. Usually, the cost is listed per square foot of the material. When comparing countertop costs, check whether the estimate is for the material with installation, or just the material. Below are some countertop materials to consider:

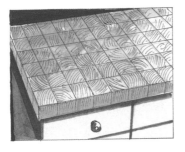

BUTCHER BLOCKS are made up of narrow strips of hardwood, typically maple, and stand up to all sorts of cutting and chopping. As the name suggests, the original butcher blocks were made for cutting meat. Butcher blocks can scratch and will burn with direct heat, but that can also be part of their charm. It's possible to sand down scratched butcher block to restore it, and there are different ways to finish it.

If the surface is frequently used for chopping and cutting, it should be oiled regularly to avoid cracking and splitting. For butcher block on an area that won't get much chopping, a varnish is recommended, as it requires less maintenance. End-grain butcher block (pictured here) has a distinctive look: the wood boards run vertically, so the surface shows the cross sections of the wood. The opposite is edge-grain, where the boards run horizontally, the long way. Butcher block should be kept dry and clean. It has a warm, old-fashioned country look.

CERAMIC TILES resist heat, scratching, and stains, although the grout between the tiles can stain. The main disadvantage to a tile countertop is that it's not level, so you can't roll dough out on it, and

items might tip over. The tile can chip; it is also very hard, so a fragile item dropped on tile is likely to break. Ceramic tiles are not practical for a countertop, but they are great on a backsplash and from there can bring an excellent design element into a kitchen.

CONCRETE is heat resistant and also stain resistant if it's sealed properly. Concrete countertops can either be precast and then cut to size, or they can be cast onsite. Pigments of any color can be mixed into the concrete, making it incredibly versatile; it can also be customized by pressing objects like shells into the wet concrete. Concrete should be rubbed with a paste-wax and resealed periodically; check with the installers about what they recommend. A concrete countertop will develop hairline cracks over time.

COPPER is a metal that is known to be a superb conductor of heat and electricity. It can be used for countertops in sheet metal form and has a warm reddish color that suits a country kitchen or a rustic look. As with other metal countertops, it's possible to have an integral sink that is part of the countertop. Copper sheets are measured in gauges, according to how thick they are; the lower the gauge number, the thicker the sheet. A countertop should be 14 to 16 gauge, while a backsplash can be thinner, around 18 to 22 gauge, for example. Copper tarnishes and develops a patina over time—think of the difference in color between a new penny and an old one. It can be treated to resist this tarnishing and waxed periodically to preserve the finish. Be aware that acidic substances like lemon juice and ketchup can discolor the surface. Cutting boards must be used on copper to avoid scratching, and pans straight from the oven can damage the surface, so trivets should be used. Like stainless steel, copper will scratch with use over time. Hammered copper is an alternative to flat metal and gives texture to the surface. Besides a kitchen counter, copper also works well in a pantry or a built-in bar area.

ENAMELED LAVA STONE countertops are made by a French company called Pyrolave, which takes volcanic stone mined in France and enamels it for a smooth surface. The product, which is relatively expensive, is available in an array of rich, deep colors. It is durable, low maintenance, and comes in either tiles or slabs.

ENGINEERED STONE is created with bits of stone, called aggregate, that are mixed with a resin and pigments. The mixture is almost all stone and is known for requiring little maintenance. The product varies from manufacturer to manufacturer, and its strength and maintenance depend on the type of stone used. Many engineered stone countertops are made using quartz or granite; both are extremely strong. Engineered stone countertops come in a wide variety of colors and are generally less expensive than natural stone. Details such as the profile of the edge will help determine the look.

GLASS countertops are made with tempered glass and are typically 1½ inches, or more, thick. They come in an assortment of colors and textures and have a clean contemporary look. Tempered glass can withstand high temperatures, so it's handy installed near a cooktop or oven. Since glass is nonporous, it requires little maintenance and is easy to keep clean. However, like ceramic tiles and some stone, glass will crack or chip if something heavy is dropped onto it; also, fingerprints show up readily on glass. This is a relatively expensive, modern-looking choice.

GRANITE is a hard and very durable igneous rock, produced deep below the earth's surface under tremendous heat and pressure. It typically contains the minerals feldspar, mica, and quartz and is available in a range of colors. Since granite is extremely hard, any glass dropped onto its surface will probably break. It's heat resistant and doesn't scratch easily, but the stone will absorb odors and oils and should be sealed; some maintenance is required to reseal it periodically. Granite has been trendy and works with a variety of looks; it can be quite contemporary and sleek when paired with stainless steel. It's important to see the actual granite slabs you're getting, as the color and quality can vary widely.

LAMINATE countertops have a layer of synthetic material affixed to a backing, such as plywood. Formica is one well-known brand name of laminates. This is an economical, durable, and versatile countertop choice that is offered in many colors and patterns. Laminates will scratch and burn, so care must be taken to use cutting boards and trivets. Water can seep into seams in the laminate, too, causing it to peel, so be sure to mop up any water. Laminates can't be sanded and refinished the way other materials like solid synthetics and wood can, but they are also less expensive to replace. Laminates can have a retro look and also work in a thoroughly contemporary kitchen. The edge of laminate countertops can be finished with a different material, such as metal or a strip of wood, to vary the look; for example, an aluminum edge on a laminate countertop has a 1950s feel, and a wood edge on a laminate countertop lends itself to a country look.

LIMESTONE is a sedimentary rock composed of accumulated bits of shell and other organic materials, mostly calcium carbonate. Limestone comes in several warm neutral colors; its beautiful, subtle hues complement either a traditional kitchen or a very modern one. It's not as hard as granite and can stain from acidic foods such as lemon juice. Limestone is relatively porous and must be sealed every so often; ask suppliers how to seal it, and how frequently. Be sure to look at the limestone slabs prior to ordering, as the color and quality can vary from slab to slab.

MARBLE is a beautiful, top-of-the-line choice for countertops. Historically, some of the finest houses had marble countertops and backsplashes. One particularly lovely and popular type is Carrara marble, which is white with gray streaks and markings, but there are many other beautiful varieties that come in an array of colors. For those who like to bake, a marble slab in the kitchen is good for rolling out dough because it's smooth and cool. Marble is not as hard as granite and requires sealing and regular maintenance. Marble scratches and can absorb oils, but it also develops a patina over time that can add to its elegance. Ask the supplier about the recommended sealant and how often to apply it. Also, as with any stone, look at the slabs before ordering as color and quality can vary.

PAPER-BASED countertops are an eco-friendly choice made from paper coated in resin that is baked to a strong, solid final product. They are low maintenance and durable, and the pulp for the paper is derived from trees in managed and sustainable forests. Richlite and PaperStone are two brands of paper-based countertops, both offer a choice of colors. This something to consider for any project, but in particular for one focused on keeping the environmental impact low.

MATERIALS

A big part of what architects, furniture designers, and interior designers do is to decide which materials to use in constructing and decorating a building. New materials are constantly being developed, while old standards such as brick, concrete, and stone have been used for thousands of years. Some architects are known for using materials in a certain way. Architect Frank Gehry's (b. 1929) innovative application of titanium for the exterior of buildings, such as the Guggenheim Museum in Bilbao, Spain, has caused a splash, for example.

Different materials have different properties. Some are very hard, while others are soft. Some can withstand huge amounts of compression, while others can support a lot of weight while spanning an opening. Some will crack in cold weather, and others withstand the cold. Much of designing a building is choosing the right materials by taking into account their look, cost, life expectancy, and suitability for the job.

SLATE is typically a blue-gray color, but may also be brown, green, or even have purple tones. This stone is fine-grained and splits on parallel planes. Slate is not as porous as granite and marble, which means it's less likely to stain. It is also heat resistant and is a durable choice; it will need to be oiled occasionally. Slate has a matte appearance, which can be waxed to make it glossier.

SOAPSTONE is comprised of talc, chlorite, and quartz; it starts out a light gray color but darkens to a rich hue as it oxidizes. Nonporous and impervious to stains, it is the material of choice for science lab countertops, as it stands up to heat and won't absorb oils and liquids the way granite and marble can. Soapstone has to be treated with mineral oil regularly when it's new. It can dent, but typically won't chip or crack like harder stones. It has a soft, warm look that suits many different styles. Like other stones, soapstone is a relatively expensive choice, but where budget permits it's a great option to consider.

SOLID SYNTHETICS can be sanded to remove stains, scratches, and burns. Corian is one well-known brand; it's a relatively new material, introduced in the early 1970s, that can work with both modern and traditional styles. It comes in a range of colors and is easily contoured or curved. The profile of the edge of the countertop can help to determine its look.

STAINLESS STEEL countertops have a warm neutral color and are heat resistant. This is the countertop material typically chosen for professional kitchens. Sheets of stainless steel, like other metals, come in different thicknesses measured in gauges: a 16-gauge piece is $1/16$ inch thick, for example. The lower the gauge, the thicker the sheet. For countertops, 14- or 16-gauge stainless steel is typical. For backsplashes, the steel can be thinner—from 18 to 22 gauge. Stainless steel will scratch over time, giving it a soft patina. Since it does scratch, it's important not to clean it with abrasives. Stainless steel also comes with a buffed finish, where it is essentially prescratched; this softens the look and takes away the anxiety of the first inevitable scratches. A downside to stainless steel is that it shows fingerprints.

WOOD countertops have a wonderful warm look, and for this reason have been used in kitchens for a very long time. They are usually made with planks of wood that are stained and sealed; maple is a hardwood commonly chosen for countertops. Wood countertops scratch easily and will burn, so it's essential to use cutting boards and trivets. On the plus side, wood is a somewhat soft surface, so if a glass falls onto the countertop, it's not as likely to break as it would with a ceramic tile, stone, or concrete countertop. A wood countertop can have an old-fashioned appeal; stained a medium brown, it can be perfect for a country kitchen. A favorite look combines a medium brown wood countertop with a ceramic tile backsplash.

ZINC is a metal with a warm bluish color that is often chosen for bars and countertops in restaurants—the look of zinc is a staple of the classic French bistro. Zinc is beautiful but also expensive. It will oxidize and develop a patina unless it is regularly waxed and polished. Some people will prefer the look of oxidized zinc and decide not to polish it. Like other metals, zinc will scratch and can be damaged by intense heat. When budget permits, it offers a more mellow and complex color than stainless steel, and has a country look. For a built-in bar area, a zinc countertop would be a classic choice.

Floor and wall coverings in a kitchen should be easy to clean and maintain. There are so many choices that it's best to start by thinking about what colors and textures you like. Your budget will help to determine what choices you make; for example, a coat of paint on the walls and vinyl floor tiles will be a relatively inexpensive option whereas wallpaper on the walls and hardwood floors will typically be more expensive.

In the old days, **KITCHEN FLOORS** were likely to be packed earth or stone. Today, the one material you probably don't want on a kitchen floor is carpeting. Otherwise, anything goes, as long as it's easy to clean and durable. One consideration is that hard surfaces such as stone, concrete, and ceramic tile will be harder on your feet and your back than more resilient materials such as wood, bamboo, cork, linoleum, or vinyl. If you spend a lot of time standing in the kitchen, this is something to bear in mind.

Surfaces such as wood and cork should have a polyurethane finish for easy maintenance. This helps to protect the floor against staining. Spills on a wood or cork floor could cause damage and so should be cleaned up quickly and not left to sit. A painted wood floor is perfect for a country kitchen. Linoleum was an old standard before vinyl replaced it in popularity in the 1940s. It's made a comeback in recent years, partly because it's considered a natural material that is an option for green design. The ingredients in linoleum include linseed oil, powdered wood, ground limestone, resins, dying agents, and pigments—all natural materials considered more eco-friendly than other man-made ones. Cork tiles are a particular favorite in the kitchen, as they are easy on the feet and have a warm color.

KITCHEN WALLS can be painted, wallpapered, tiled, or covered any way you want. Paint with a satin finish is a good choice in the kitchen, as it's easier to clean than flat paint. If you choose wallpaper for the kitchen walls and want to continue it over the backsplash, a ¼-inch thick piece of glass should be installed to protect it.

Kitchen lighting is critical for making the best use of the room. Direct light, called task lighting, is necessary over work spaces such as the sink, cooktop, and food preparation areas. Background lighting, or ambient lighting, fills the room with indirect light. If possible, have lights on dimmers, especially in an open plan that incorporates dining and living areas; it's best when the lights in separate areas can be turned on and off independently, which allows for more control over the mood of the room. Try to maximize the use of natural light through windows and skylights. And remember: it's always nice to have a window over a kitchen sink.

Fluorescent light, whether in tubes or bulbs, is an energy-efficient choice. Fluorescent bulbs, or tubes, with warm light are preferred over those with bluish, cooler light. Fixtures with halogen bulbs are another popular choice; they are more energy-efficient than regular incandescent bulbs and have a clear light close to the color of natural sunlight. A drawback to halogen lights is that they generate a lot of heat. Xenon bulbs have xenon gas in them and provide a warm colored light that is similar to incandescent bulbs. The variety of lighting options is huge, but a few basics are as follows:

LOW-VOLTAGE LIGHTING, a popular choice for kitchens, has a transformer that brings the voltage down from the standard 110 volts of most household outlets. Halogen bulbs are often used with low-voltage lighting; they are very bright and get quite hot. The fixtures are typically recessed into the ceiling or come as track lighting. They offer savings on electricity as well as optimal levels of light.

PENDANT LIGHT FIXTURES hang down from the ceiling and provide direct light onto a surface, which is great for a kitchen. A pendant light fixture can be used alone or might be grouped in a row of three or more. Typical locations include over a dining table or illuminating a kitchen island or peninsula. Pendant lights are hung about 2 feet over a countertop. If there are a few in a row, the areas of light from each fixture should overlap, so that the light is continuous.

UNDER-CABINET LIGHTING has fixtures secured underneath the kitchen cabinets to illuminate the countertops—key in a kitchen, because this provides direct light for working. These fixtures can be either wired directly or plugged into an electrical outlet. Ideally, they are concealed behind the lip of the upper cabinet. They are easy to install, as long as there is an available source of electricity. Small round lights, sometimes called puck lights, can be affixed to the

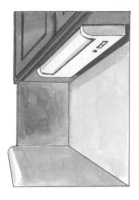

underside of the kitchen cabinets. Like other fixtures, they can be wired directly or plugged in; in addition, some models are battery operated, which makes installation quite easy. They can be stuck with adhesive or screwed into the underside of the cabinet, depending on the model. Installing under-cabinet lighting is a relatively easy pick-me-up for a dark kitchen, and it's essential for any new kitchens. During a party, or just a dinner at home, dimming or turning off the ceiling fixtures in the kitchen and leaving on the under-cabinet lights can create a nice ambience.

Kitchen sinks are probably the most-used element of the kitchen, the main point in a work triangle that also comprises the cooktop and refrigerator (see p. 87). The sink should be placed near a dishwasher for convenience; a larger kitchen might accommodate two sinks.

Early kitchen sinks were made from a slab of stone or constructed with a thin sheet of metal over a wood frame. Today, designs for kitchen sinks vary greatly, with materials ranging from stainless steel to enameled cast iron to copper. A sink can be oversized, but the standard size is approximately 22 by 26 inches. The depth varies, with the standard being 7 or 8 inches; for big pots and pans, it can be convenient to have a deep sink of 10 inches or more. A deeper sink will also minimize the amount of water that splashes out.

Kitchen sinks can be drop-in or undermount (see p. 147). In a kitchen, it's easier to keep an undermount sink clean, as crumbs can be swept directly off the counter into the sink. With a drop-in sink, also known as a self-rimming sink, the rim prevents a clean sweep from countertop into sink and crumbs get stuck on the rim.

Drop-in sinks come with openings cut into them for faucets and accessories. If there are extra holes in the sink, they can be used for a vegetable sprayer, water filter, or instant hot water dispenser, for example; otherwise, they can be plugged with caps. An undermount sink has faucets and accessories either installed in the countertop or wall mounted. Kitchen sinks typically have strainer drains (as pictured on p. 137).

BAR SINKS are usually smaller and more decorative than utilitarian kitchen sinks, and are good for a bar area or pantry. A copper sink combined with a black stone or brown wood countertop would be an interesting look. There are nickel and zinc sinks as well, which all have classic appeal; a small stainless steel sink might also be used in a bar. Gooseneck spouts, which arch up high, are handy for bar sinks, as they allow you to easily fill a pitcher of water.

Sinks with **DOUBLE BOWLS** allow for one bowl to be filled with dirty dishes and the other to be used for preparing food and rinsing dishes. This is a great convenience if you've got the space. In some styles, the second bowl is much smaller than the primary bowl; this is a good option if space is limited. Double-bowl sinks also help to conserve water: fill one bowl with water and some soap to soak dirty dishes, then scrub them with the same water and rinse with fresh water over the other bowl. This means not having the water running from the tap the entire time the dishes are being washed.

FARM SINKS, also called **FRONT APRON PANEL SINKS,** have a front vertical panel and a distinctive country look. This type of sink is typically undermounted on three sides, meaning the sink fits just under the countertop and, unlike with other styles, there is no countertop material along the sink's front edge. These are generally large rectangular sinks that offer a lot of room and can be divided into two separate bowls.

FAUCETS for a kitchen sink can have either separate handles for hot and cold water, or a single handle that controls both temperature and water pressure. When your hands are covered in flour and you've got a pot in one hand and a carrot in the other, it's easier to use a single lever handle than two separate handles. Two separate handles, however, provide more control over the temperature and water pressure.

POT-FILLING FAUCETS are used to fill pots of water without having to haul the brimming pot from sink to cooktop. This faucet is typically wall mounted over a range or a cooktop and extends out from the wall, though it can also be installed into the countertop. A pot-filling faucet requires that a water supply line be run to the cooking area.

PULLDOWN SPRAY FAUCETS, also called **PULLOUT SPRAY FAUCETS,** have a sprayer at the business end of the spout that can be pulled out for more control and leverage. The sprayer acts as a regular spout when in place, but when extended provides a better angle for washing a big pot, for example. An alternative is a hand spray, which is separate from the sink spout.

HAND SPRAYS, also called **VEGETABLE SPRAYS,** are pullout spray nozzles convenient for washing pots and even for cleaning the sink, since they can be angled in any direction. When in use, the hand spray diverts water from the faucet.

KITCHEN SINK MATERIALS run the gamut from the common stainless steel and enameled cast iron to the rarer copper and nickel varieties. A sink can be made of any material that stands up to exposure to water and wear and tear. Stainless steel sinks should be 20 gauge or lower; the lower the gauge, the thicker the sheet of steel. Stainless steel sinks that are coated on the underside will help to muffle the sound of water hitting the metal, and this is recommended.

Enameled cast iron has a great old-fashioned look and comes in a variety of colors. One drawback is that the enamel can chip if a heavy pot is dropped onto it. A grille placed on the bottom of enameled cast-iron sinks can protect them against this. These grilles are often sold with the sinks in complementary colors.

The sink material may match that of the countertop. Copper, zinc, and solid synthetic countertops can all have integral sinks, meaning the sink is a part of them. A copper sink has a country look; it goes well in a bar or a pantry.

Centuries ago, sinks were often made out of a slab of stone, and this is still possible today. A stone sink can be custom-made with a few slabs of stone sealed together.

Pantries, also called **BUTLER'S PANTRIES**, are small rooms between kitchens and dining rooms where traditionally food was prepared for presentation before serving. Table settings and serving plates were also stored here. Today they can still provide additional storage space, a surface for serving food or drinks from, as well as extra counter space for cooking or preparing food. The word pantry comes from the Latin word *panis* meaning "bread." Older houses often have pantries. Typically, they included cabinets, counter space, and a small sink; formal place settings were stored here, apart from the utilitarian plates, glasses, and so forth in the kitchen. An old-fashioned pantry might have wood countertops, glass-paned cabinet doors, bin pulls (see p. 64), and cabinet latches on white- or black-painted cabinets.

Storage is critical to a kitchen that functions well, because the kitchen in particular is a room that should be highly organized. When building or renovating a kitchen, give ample thought, while looking at the plans, to where items will go and how accessible they will be. For example, a garbage bin should be close to the kitchen sink and dishwasher; this makes peeling vegetables before dinner or scraping plates after more convenient.

GARBAGE AND RECYCLING STORAGE should be located somewhere that is convenient but also out of sight. If a dishwasher is on one side of the kitchen sink, garbage bins are well placed either under the sink or on the opposite side of it. Having double bins is par-

ticularly convenient: one can be for garbage, and the other for recycling. A garbage bin under the sink or counter-top can be mounted on heavy-duty glides so that it pulls out easily. Garbage bins should be big enough to get through a whole day—or at least an entire dinner—before requiring emptying.

bathrooms

THERE'S NO QUESTION that bathrooms are absolutely necessary rooms, but when possible a bathroom should be not just a functional room, but a relaxing oasis removed from the hectic pace of modern life. It will improve your state of mind, and possibly increase the resale value of the property. Put lights on dimmers, use colors and materials that you love, and plan on a bathtub if there is space for it.

Some of the earliest-known indoor bathrooms were built approximately 3,500 years ago at the royal palace of Knossos on the island of Crete. These were remarkable and extremely sophisticated, with running water, bathtubs, and flushing toilets.

Bathroom design has not been consistently progressive since then. The Middle Ages in Europe—from the sixth to the fifteenth centuries AD—were a barbaric age, particularly on the bathroom front. Chamber pots were the norm. As centuries went by, however, technology developed, plumbing improved, and by the late nineteenth century the modernized bathroom had become a status symbol—as it still is today.

When planning a bathroom renovation, keep in mind that moving plumbing fixtures like toilets, basins, and bathtubs entails expensive construction. It's much more economical to replace fixtures without changing the plumbing lines. If you want a larger bathroom but have a budget to consider, think about expanding the room but leaving the fixtures where they are.

Bathroom accessories keep a bathroom neat and organized; they give everything from toothbrushes to towels a place. If you have a freestanding sink, which lacks the counter and storage space that a vanity provides, glass shelves, extra towel bars, and other accessories will be particularly useful.

If a bathroom wall is tiled, it's possible to drill into the tile to install new accessories such as towel bars; the drill must have the proper bit for tile. The metal finish of accessories, such as towel bars, should match the metal of the fittings, such as the faucets and tub spouts; glass, ceramics, or plastic accessories can be mixed with any metal fittings.

CLOTHES HAMPERS may be built-in or freestanding and are important not to overlook when designing a bathroom. Any bathroom that is big enough should have a hamper for used clothes and towels. A hamper can be built into a vanity as a drawer or door that pulls out. There are also many attractive freestanding hampers to choose from; in a country-style bathroom, try a big basket with a lid.

A **GLASS SHELF** (or wood or ceramic shelf) is a great space saver and is especially handy  when there is a freestanding sink and therefore not a lot of storage space. A glass shelf typically goes above the basin and under the medicine cabinet or mirror. If there's no medicine cabinet and only a mirror, all the more reason to consider a shelf. Shelves come in sizes of about 12 to 24 inches wide and 3 to 6 inches deep. They can be installed into tile or wall, be it wallboard or plaster. One practical consideration: it can be annoying to have a shelf over a toilet, because if something falls off the shelf it may land in the toilet. Some glass shelves come with a rail to prevent this from happening.

HOOKS are particularly practical in a bathroom. Every bathroom door should have at least one hook on the back for a bathrobe or a towel. Hooks can help keep damp towels and clothes off the floor. They come in a variety of styles, from übermodern to thoroughly traditional; choose hooks to match the finish and style of the other bathroom fittings and accessories.

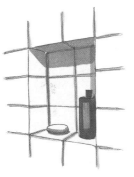

RECESSED NICHES in bathtub and shower enclosures are best when they are tall enough to hold a shampoo bottle or two as well as a soap dish. Adding a recessed niche is something to consider if you are retiling or redoing a bathroom. A niche can be at bathtub level with the bottom of the niche at about 20 to 25 inches from the floor depending on the depth of the bathtub, or shower level, with the bottom of the niche about 48 inches from the floor. The depth is usually 3 to 4 inches. Two recessed niches—one at bathtub height and the other at shower height—is a nice option.

SHAVING MIRRORS provide a close-up view for shaving, plucking, or plain old admiring. They are installed into tile or wall. Some models spring out from the wall and swing so that you can maneuver them to the right spot. Mount a shaving mirror as close to the basin as possible so that water is readily accessible. Also, having the shaving mirror near the basin mirror allows you to check out the side or back of your head. Their old-fashioned look also works well in a bathroom with a contemporary design.

SOAP DISHES can be either surface mounted or recessed into the wall. New soap dishes added to existing bathrooms are typically surface mounted because recessing them involves more work. For a bathtub with a showerhead, consider adding surface-mounted soap dishes at different levels—one convenient for taking a bath and the other for showering. There are many styles to choose from; one favorite is the corner-mounted wire soap dish installed on the wall over tile (as pictured here). This style drains well so the soap doesn't get mushy, and it comes in a variety of sizes. A recessed ceramic soap dish, which is common in older bathrooms, has an old-fashioned look.

TOILET PAPER HOLDERS can be recessed into the wall or surface mounted, as pictured here. Surface-mounted toilet paper holders have either a single post or a double post, meaning they attach to the wall in either one or two places. A single post has an arm that goes through the roll, while the double post operates on a spring mechanism. A toilet paper holder, recessed or surface mounted, should be installed approximately 22 inches from the floor. When deciding on the location for the toilet paper holder, don't forget that it can be mounted onto or recessed into the side of a vanity to save space.

TOOTHBRUSH HOLDERS can be either mounted onto the wall by the basin or freestanding on a vanity countertop or a shelf. These days, toothbrushes are thicker than they used to be, so some won't fit into an older holder. If you like big, chunky toothbrushes, investigate the size of the holder's holes before mounting a new one onto the wall or deciding to keep the old one in a renovation.

TOWEL BARS are standard issue for bathrooms. There is no hard and fast rule for what height to hang them on the wall, but the average is about 48 inches from the floor. That said, a towel bar mounted 58 to 62 inches from the ground allows space for big bath towels to hang without coming too close to the floor. Alternatively, in a small bathroom placing a towel bar only 40 to 44 inches from the floor can help make the ceiling seem higher. For bathrooms without a lot of wall space, towel bars can be hung on the wall one over another. Towel bars come in a variety of widths, ranging from about 18 to 32 inches; wider ones can hold two bath towels side by side. A towel bar is best placed so that you can reach a towel from the bathtub or shower. Early towel bars were made with wood, and today a bathroom with a retro look might have a wood bar with built-in ceramic brackets. **DOUBLE TOWEL BARS** feature two parallel bars as part of the same unit. These are useful in a small space. The following are some other variations:

An **ESCUTCHEON,** pronounced "es-skuch-en," is a protective as well as decorative plate on a wall or door surface that surrounds a keyhole, towel bar, plumbing fixture, or doorknob, for example. The word comes from the Latin word scutum, meaning "shield." An escutcheon helps to cover minor damage from installing such items—for instance, if a tile is chipped a bit when a new towel bar is drilled into tile wall.

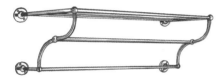

HOTEL-STYLE TOWEL RACKS are designed to hold a stack of folded towels in addition to accommodating hanging towels. As the name suggests, they are frequently used in hotel bathrooms where storage space is limited. This style offers a great solution in bathrooms without space for a vanity or built-in storage. Typically a hotel-style towel rack is mounted on the wall higher than a regular towel rack, but not so high that it's difficult to reach the towels.

TOWEL RINGS are practical in a tight spot where there isn't room for a full towel bar. A towel ring can be added to the side of a vanity for hand towels, or a few of them can be installed in a row on the wall for bath towels. As with the towel bar, there's no hard and fast rule for what height to install a towel ring; just keep in mind that the top of the hanging towel will be several inches lower than the point where the base of the ring is mounted. How high you hang it also depends on how you plan to use it. On the wall by a basin in a powder room, a towel ring should be 42 to 52 inches from the floor to the center of the back plate. If you're using a towel ring for a bath towel, hang it higher.

TOWEL WARMERS can be used to store towels, like towel bars, in addition to heating and drying them. Towel warmers can be electric or connected to a building's hot water system. An electric towel warmer is easier to install, as it requires only an electrical outlet, and is often freestanding. Hot-water-heated towel bars require a plumbing line and can be placed near a bathtub. An electric towel warmer should not be installed too close to the tub, to avoid the risk of electric shock.

Bathroom lighting is usually a combination of ceiling fixtures for ambient light and wall-mounted fixtures for direct light. There should be direct light by mirrors, or any place where people might put on makeup or shave. Ideally, there will also be a recessed ceiling fixture over a shower, particularly if light doesn't come through the shower door or curtain. Consider a light for over the bathtub as well, especially if someone loves to read in the tub. Waterproof light fixtures, which are designed for use in wet locations, are often required for lighting in shower stalls and over bathtubs. Be sure all bathroom lights have dimmers, to ensure a relaxing low-light bath experience. Dimmed lights also create a nice ambience in a powder room when you have guests.

A **CEILING LIGHT** provides ambient light for larger bathrooms; a small or half bathroom likely will only require wall-mounted light fixtures. Because overhead light is not very flattering, a ceiling fixture—whether it's recessed, track, or a chandelier—should not be the only light source over a mirror. Ideally, there would also be wall-mounted fixtures above or on either side of the mirror. Changing fixtures for a quick spruce up is relatively easy, whereas moving light fixtures requires much more work, as the wiring in the wall will have to be moved as well. Building codes frequently require that a bathroom with no windows be vented, and exhaust fans, which are often installed into the ceiling for this purpose, are available with lights. However, it's best to keep the bathroom vent and ceiling light separate, so that you can turn only one on as needed. Some ceiling light options include the following:

SURFACE-MOUNTED CEILING LIGHT FIXTURES are installed directly on the ceiling, usually in the center of the room. These fixtures come in a huge variety of styles, but the classic bathroom surface-mounted ceiling fixture has a white-toned glass or plastic globe that conceals and mutes the direct glare of the bulbs. Alternatives are recessed fixtures, sometimes called high-hats, and track lighting.

CHANDELIERS can be an elegant and distinctive touch in a bathroom. Unlike a surface-mounted ceiling fixture, a chandelier hangs down off the ceiling, adding sparkle to the room. The same wiring requirements exist as with any ceiling light fixture, and it's a good idea to check whether additional support is needed in the ceiling to hold the chandelier's weight. A chandelier requires a high ceiling to ensure sufficient clearance; seven feet is generally the minimum amount of space under a chandelier. Its size should be scaled to that of the bathroom; a small chandelier works for a smallish bathroom, for example. Designs are quite varied. A crystal chandelier provides an elegant look, whereas an antler hanging fixture would lend itself to a rustic look; a tole hanging fixture, which is made of painted metal, works with almost any style.

SKYLIGHTS are limited, of course, to rooms without finished space over them. Where possible, a skylight can be a great addition to a bathroom (or to any room). In an interior bathroom with no windows, a skylight will let in loads of natural light while still offering privacy. Also, sunlight pouring down from a skylight above can literally warm up ceramic tile, stone, and similar materials typically used in a bathroom. Taking advantage of natural light is also a good way to cut down on electricity consumption. However, keep in mind that in hot climates with few cloudy days, a skylight can create an uncomfortable glare from too much direct sunlight and also may overheat the room. To avoid these problems, some skylights come with a coating on the glass to minimize the glare and heat; others are designed to diffuse the light coming in, or have shades to block the sunlight. The skylight's size can also help to determine how much heat and glare come in. Installing a skylight involves some construction; the scope of the work depends on the structure of the house and the size of the skylight.

VANITY LIGHTING illuminates the mirror over a vanity, washstand, or basin. The light fixtures are mounted on the wall, typically either above or on each side of the mirror for flattering illumination. Ideal lighting is provided by wall sconces on either side of the mirror, hung 66 to 70 inches from the floor to the center of the fixture. Vanity lighting should be used even if there is a ceiling light fixture, as a ceiling light alone creates unflattering shadows on the faces of those using the mirror. In a small bathroom or half bathroom, wall-mounted fixtures may be all that is needed.

THEATRICAL LIGHTING FIXTURES are strips of round exposed bulbs that surround the vanity mirror. Theatrical lighting provides lots of light and few shadows on the face, which is why movie stars like to have it in their dressing rooms for applying makeup. It's possible to install theatrical lighting strips just along the top or along the sides of a mirror.

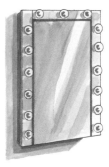

Bathtubs have been around for thousands of years. The ancient Romans were known for their elaborate public baths, where people went to socialize, soak, and steam; the Baths of Caracalla in Rome, for example, were built in the early third century AD to accommodate up to 1,600 people at a time. Today, communal bathing is still a part of social life in countries such as Turkey, Iceland, and Japan.

In American culture, however, bathing is more of an intimate than a social activity. The bath is generally thought of as a place for relaxation, and most tubs are designed for one person. There are many styles of bathtubs, and it's a good idea to sit in a tub before you buy it. The pitch of the back varies; a straight vertical back won't be as comfortable as a curved, sloped back. The length of a tub is critical, too, to ensure it will fit in the bathroom. Five to five-and-a-half feet are standard lengths, although longer ones are available. Tub depth should also be considered. The standard is approximately 14 to 17 inches, but it's relaxing—decadent as well—to have a deeper tub. Luxury bathtubs are available with depths of 20 inches or more. However, if you're considering this option, make sure that your hot water heater can fill a deep tub; it would be incredibly frustrating to have such a tub and not enough hot water to fill it.

In addition, when installing a new tub, check with an engineer that your floor can support the weight when it's full of water; you might need to add support under the floor. If you're installing a new bathtub in an existing house, also be sure that it's possible to get the tub into the bathroom—especially if there's a curved staircase involved. Keep the weight in mind as well: a cast-iron bathtub weighs hundreds of pounds and can be difficult to carry up several flights of stairs. If you dislike the color of an existing bathtub, it can be changed by refinishing it—this is much less expensive than buying and installing a new tub.

The tub spout, faucet handles, and overflow can be at one end of the tub or in the center; either way, the plumbing in the wall must correspond to the configuration of the bathtub. For safety, consider mounting a grab bar on the wall over a bathtub; there are some attractive styles available, and for anyone—of any age—it can prevent a fall.

AIR BATHS blow small bubbles of warmed air from the bottom of the tub. An air bath doesn't target specific achy joints like the jets in a whirlpool bathtub do, but it provides an allover massage. Like a whirlpool, this is a specific type of bathtub that has an air bath mechanism built into it. In some cases, the motor for the air bath can be installed a short distance from the tub to make for a quiet bathing experience. Installation of an air bath requires electrical wiring and an access panel as specified by the manufacturer; also, check with the manufacturer on recommended maintenance for an air bath. For the ultimate bathing experience, combination air bath and whirlpool systems are available.

CORNER BATHTUBS can be triangular in shape or have five sides with a flat front. They are designed to fit into the corner, and offer a compact option for bathrooms that won't take a rectangular tub. Typically, corner bathtubs are made of acrylic, which is easier to mold than materials such as cast iron. One disadvantage to corner tubs is that they can be difficult to clean, as you have to get into them to reach the corners. With certain bathroom layouts, though, a corner bathtub is an excellent solution.

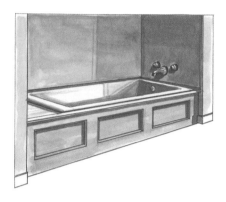

DECK-MOUNTED BATHTUBS have a frame that surrounds and supports the tub. Either a drop-in or an undermount bathtub can be installed into the frame (see p. 141 for a comparison of drop-in versus undermount styles). The deck is the horizontal platform around the tub. If it's wide enough, it can be used as a place to store soap, candles, shampoo bottles, and other items. The deck should be a minimum of 6 inches and no greater than 10 inches wide. The deck must be of a waterproof material such as stone or ceramic tile; the vertical surfaces of the frame may be covered in the same waterproof material or a wood panel. A removable panel is required for access to the plumbing. A deck-mounted bathtub may take up more space than a bathtub with an integral apron, and construction of the frame can be more labor intensive, and therefore expensive. However, the surface surrounding the bathtub is convenient for storing bath items and can make getting into and out of the bathtub easier.

FREESTANDING BATHTUBS are finished on all sides and stand on their own either by a wall or in the middle of a room. Before installing a deluxe freestanding bathtub, consult an engineer to make sure that the floor joists (the structural elements in a floor) will be able to support the tub when it's full of water. If the joists aren't strong enough, a beam or some other support might have to be added. If the tub is in the center of the bathroom, the fittings, which include the faucet handles and tub spout, will have to be floor mounted, and the plumbing lines will be run through the floor instead of through the wall, which is more common. Freestanding bathtubs come in a wide variety of styles; a couple of classic examples include the following:

CLAW-FOOT BATHTUBS, with their four supporting feet, are decidedly old-fashioned looking. Traditionally, claw-foot tubs are made of cast iron and have a rolled rim. Typically, one end of the tub is flat and houses the tub spout and faucet handles, while the other end is rounded. However, some are rounded on both ends, allowing you to recline either way. When both ends are rounded, fittings such as the spout and drain are in the center of the tub. Vintage tubs are available, along with new reproductions. If you are fixing up an older house, a claw-foot tub can help achieve a period look. Claw-foot tubs can look at home in a modern house as well. However, keep in mind that small children and elderly people may find it difficult to climb into and out of these tubs. In addition, showering in a claw-foot tub can be less than ideal, as the bottom of the tub is slightly curved and water tends to splash out on all sides.

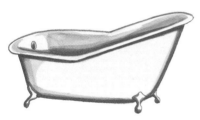

SLIPPER BATHTUBS have one end that rises up higher than the other; double slipper bathtubs have both ends raised. The higher end of this style supports full-fledged lounging. The spout and faucet handles will typically be at the lower end or, if it's a double slipper tub with two raised ends, the spout and fittings will typically be in the center. It's a classic design; a bathtub found at the royal palace of Knossos on the island of Crete dating from approximately 3,500 years ago had a raised end like a slipper tub. A slipper bathtub will be a statement in a bathroom.

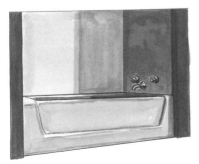

INTEGRAL APRON BATHTUBS have a built-in vertical panel from the top of the tub rim to the floor. This panel is known as the apron, or sometimes skirting, and is an integral part of the bathtub. Without the apron, the

REFINISHING A BATHTUB is a lot less expensive and much less disruptive than replacing it. The tub stays right where it is and gets a fresh new look—like giving a wall a fresh coat of paint. If a bathtub has chips in the porcelain or brown stains from a long-term drip, then it's a candidate for refinishing. To preserve an original claw-foot tub, refinishing is the best option. If the bathtub is a hideous color, refinishing can allow you to choose one you like. There are a few different ways to refinish a tub, and it's best to discuss the options with the refinisher. Much will depend on the bathtub's material.

underside of the tub and the gaps between the bathtub and the walls would be visible. The apron may be ordered separately from the tub, which offers more options for the material and finish. Bathtubs either have a finished apron on one side running the length of the tub, for installation in an alcove, or they have two finished sides running the length and one end of the tub, for installation in a corner. This kind of tub generally takes up less space than a deck-mounted one and is less expensive, since the installation does not require building and finishing a support framework.

For bathtubs, **MATERIALS** may vary from marble to copper to stainless steel, but the standard options include enameled cast iron, enameled steel, acrylic, and fiberglass. The most timeless and longest lasting choice is enameled cast iron, which has been used for bathtubs since about 1870. It has a substantial feel and won't sound hollow when you knock against it, but it can be expensive. A cast-iron tub frequently comes with a lifetime guarantee. However, it's also heavy and can chip over time. Enameled steel is lighter than cast iron and generally less expensive, but it has a less substantial feel. Both types are finished in porcelain enameling, also called vitreous enameling, which is a thin layer of glass fused onto the metal of a tub, giving it a smooth surface and preventing corrosion. Tubs with complex shapes are usually made of acrylic, which can be molded into more complicated shapes than cast iron or steel; it is known to hold heat well and is much lighter than cast iron. Some acrylic tubs also contain fiberglass for reinforcement. A layer of concrete, called a concrete pan, can be installed under an acrylic bathtub to prevent it from sounding hollow when you step into it. No matter which material you choose, be sure to check which cleansers are recommended to avoid scratching or damaging the tub.

PREFABRICATED BATHTUB AND SHOWER COMBINATION UNITS are comprised of a bathtub and a shower enclosure, offering an inexpensive alternative to installing a bathtub and tiling the surrounding walls. Typically, they come in one unit, which is too big to fit through a doorway or up a staircase. Because it is nearly impossible to get most units into a finished house or building, they are generally only useful in a space that's being built. It's possible, however, to find prefab bathtub and shower combos that are made in two pieces, which should fit into a finished building. Clearly this is something to investigate before ordering the unit.

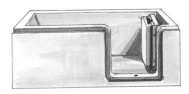

WALK-IN BATHTUBS have doors for easy access, as well as a low step to get into them and an integral seat. They are recommended mainly for the elderly, handicapped, or anyone who has trouble getting into and out of a conventional tub. This tub can be used in conjunction with a showerhead or handheld shower. Some models come with jets, like a whirlpool bath, which adds to the hydrotherapy experience.

WHIRLPOOL BATHTUBS have jets that can be aimed at an achy back. Roy Jacuzzi invented the first self-contained whirlpool bathtub in 1968, which is why they are sometimes referred to as "Jacuzzis." A whirlpool bathtub uses an electric pump to circulate water from the tub and through the jets. These bathtubs are generally deep and require a lot of hot water to fill them. Bubble bath and bath oils can be used in a whirlpool tub only when the jets are not running; when the jets are operating, oils and such get into the plumbing, which is not recommended. These tubs need to be installed with access to the electricity and plumbing; the manufacturers will specify the electric requirements and suggested maintenance. Some whirlpool bathtubs are combined air baths, providing a decadent at-home spa experience.

Bidets, pronounced "bee-day," are bathroom fixtures for washing one's private areas. In French, the word means "pony," presumably because you sit astride a bidet to use it. Bidets are thought to have first appeared in the early eighteenth century in France and today are regularly found in Europe, South America, and parts of Asia, but rarely in the United States.

Like a toilet, a bidet is typically made with vitreous china, and has a bowl with a drain, although the bowl is shallower than a toilet bowl. It looks like a combination of a basin and a toilet. A bidet can have an "over-the-rim" spout that fills the bowl as well as a nozzle that shoots water vertically from the bowl. Some bidets also come with horizontal sprays that shoot water from the back rim of the bowl. The fixture has one or more openings precut into it for the fittings, which are the faucets, spouts, and nozzles. The bidet's design will dictate which sprays are possible to use with it. There are bidet attachments for existing toilets, which is an option if there isn't room for a separate bidet. For people with mobility issues or the elderly, bidets or the bidet attachments for toilets are recommended for good hygiene.

Drains are a necessary counterpoint for every fixture that water is released from—this includes sinks, basins, bathtubs, bidets, and showers. A floor might have a drain as well. Some drains have only a strainer; others can be controlled to hold and release water. Vintage bathtubs and basins might have only a rubber stopper to control the flow of water down a drain. Most manufacturers and retailers recom-

mend drains that work best with a certain fixture. A few different types of drains are described below:

LIFT-AND-TURN DRAINS are manually operated by lifting and rotating the center piece of the drain to release water. This may be found on a claw-foot bathtub, for example. Without a trip lever, this drain requires plunging your arm into the water to release it.

PLUNGER DRAINS have a trip lever near the overflow drain in the bathtub. This lever controls a plunger mechanism in the pipe that opens and closes the drain. Unlike a pop-up drain, there is no visible action when the trip lever is operated.

POP-UP DRAINS are used for bathtubs, sinks, and bidets. They have a lever that, when pressed down or lifted up, makes the center section of the drain go down or pop up to hold or release water, respectively.

SHOWER DRAINS are simple contraptions that don't open and close—they just have a strainer covering the drainpipe. Most shower stalls have these drains.

STRAINER DRAINS have a strainer basket that can be removed to be cleaned; they are common in kitchen sinks. The strainer basket can be secured to keep water from draining out of the sink, or left open to catch items that might clog the pipes.

Fittings refer to the spouts, lavatory sets, showerheads, hand showers, and shower controls that are needed to operate the fixtures such as the bath, shower, basin, and bidet. The style of the fittings helps to set the tone for the look of the bathroom. It's essential that the fittings correspond to the fixtures; some basins, for example, come with precut openings for lavatory sets with an 8-inch spread, meaning the overall distance from faucet handle to faucet handle is 8 inches. In this case, a lavatory set with an 8-inch spread will be required, as others simply won't fit. The "trim" refers to the decorative exposed elements, which are visible on the walls or the fixtures.

BIDET FITTINGS correlate with the design of the bidet fixture. Some bidets have just one opening precut into the deck (the horizontal area behind the bowl). In this case, the bidet requires an over-the-rim fitting (as pictured here), which is one unit with a small spout and hot and cold handles that pours water into the bowl. It's also possible to have wall-mounted handles and just a small spout mounted on the deck. Bidets with three holes on the deck require fittings with separate hot water and cold water handles. These bidets more typically have a vertical spray in the bowl, and the nozzle for this spray will be part of the fittings you need to buy.

BODY SPRAY FITTINGS are used in conjunction with a shower. Water shoots out of them in sharp bursts either from a spray bar mounted on the wall or individual spray heads (as pictured here), providing the ultimate showering experience. Body spray fittings seem to have a modern edge; however, showers in the late nineteenth century had exposed piping that surrounded the bather and sprayed water from the pipes. Body spray fittings require a water supply line in the wall.

DIVERTER VALVES direct the flow of water from one outlet to another. For instance, in a combination bathtub and shower, a diverter valve controls whether the water comes through the tub spout, the showerhead, or a hand shower. A diverter can be on a tub spout—the piece that is pulled up to change the flow of water from the spout to the showerhead. Alternatively, the diverter may be on the shower control. There are two- and three-way diverters that control the flow of water between two or three outlets.

EXPOSED SHOWER AND BATH FITTINGS
have pipes installed on the wall exterior instead of
concealed within the wall. The pipes have the same
finish as the tub spout, showerhead, and handles.
Early showers in the late nineteenth and early twentieth centuries had exposed shower and bath fittings.
Today, this is seen more often in Europe than in the
United States, and is an option to consider when
recreating a vintage or European-style bathroom.

FAUCET HANDLES con-
trol the water flow through a
spout or showerhead. Two
standard designs are the lever

handle (pictured here) and the cross handle,
with prongs (typically four of them) that radiate out from a center
piece. Lever handles are attractive and are recommended for elderly
or disabled people, as they are easier to use for those with limited grip
or mobility. There can be separate handles for hot and cold water, or a
single handle that combines both.

Handles are constructed in a few different ways. Some have
washers, but most are washerless, which is recommended. Handles
with washers are called compression handles; the washer gets
squeezed when the handle is turned and over time it will give out,
causing the handle to leak. Compression handles have separate hot
and cold handles. A washerless handle is made with a cartridge, a ball,
or a ceramic disc; most handles available today are constructed with
one of these.

FITTING FINISHES run the gamut from polished brass to bronze,
gold, chrome, or nickel. The metal finish of the fittings should be
consistent throughout the bathroom. Most fittings are made of solid
brass and plated with another material. Some finishes—brass in particular—have PVD treatment, which stands for "physical vapor depo-
sition." PVD helps to prevent tarnishing, scratching, and corrosion.
In some cases, though, you may want a finish to tarnish and develop a
patina, or glow, of age. There are some finishes, such as chrome, that
do not tarnish, so this is not an issue.

Gold finishes have a fancy ornate look, particularly if the handles
and spouts are highly detailed. The color is mellower and deeper than
that of brass. A chrome finish is a standard in bathrooms and suits

either a traditional or contemporary look, depending on the shape and design of the fittings. Chrome is quite durable and has a cool bluish color. Nickel has a soft mellow hue that is warmer than chrome; nickel fittings are a favorite, as they don't appear screamingly new and shiny. For an Arts and Crafts–style house, copper fittings are appropriate, particularly in a powder room. There are also brushed nickel and brass, which offer a softer look than the polished versions of the same. The names and subtleties of a finish vary from manufacturer to manufacturer, so it's a good idea to look at finishes in person when making a selection.

HAND SHOWERS have a small showerhead on a flexible water-resistant hose that can be moved and manipulated for extra versatility. Usually, a hand shower is mounted on the wall in a shower or stored in a cradle by a bathtub. Claw-foot bathtubs often have a hand shower in a cradle just over the tub spout and handles. Typically seen in Europe, hand showers are becoming more popular in the United States. A handheld shower is recommended for elderly or disabled people, as it can make washing easier. Whether you have kids, dogs, or just like to wash your hair in the tub, a handheld shower can be a great addition to a bathroom.

INDICES are the pieces, usually metal or porcelain, in the top of a faucet handle to indicate "hot" and "cold." They may simply read "H" or "C." Porcelain indices lend an old-fashioned sensibility to faucet handles. Some indices might say "C" or "chaud," which means hot in French or "F" or "froid," which means cold in French. Indices are typically an integral part of the handle.

LAVATORY SETS, also called **LAV SETS** or **FAUCET SETS,** are the fittings for a basin (or lavatory) and include a spout and handles. Lavatory sets typically come in 8-inch or 4-inch spreads, a spread being the measurement from the center point of one handle to the center point of the other handle, with the spout in between.

WALL MOUNTED VERSUS DECK MOUNTED

Lavatory sets, tub spouts and handles, and other fittings can either be wall mounted or deck mounted. For the most part, the choice is simply a matter of preference. Generally the design of the fixture, such as the basin or the bathtub, is for use with either deck-mounted or wall-mounted fittings, although some styles of basin or bathtub can be used with both.

WALL-MOUNTED FITTINGS are installed into the vertical surface of the wall. **DECK-MOUNTED** fittings are installed into the horizontal surface of a countertop top or fixture, such as a bidet, bathtub, or sink.

Some basins have only one opening cut into them to accommodate a single lever fitting, in which one handle mixes the hot and cold water. Other basins have no predrilled openings and are intended for use with wall-mounted or countertop-mounted lav sets. Keep in mind when choosing a lav set that the tip of a spout should never be lower than the highest possible point for the water in the basin; if the tip of the spout were to be submerged, dirty water from the basin could be sucked up the spout into the clean water supply. In addition, it's important to check that the spout on a lav set is long enough for the basin it will be paired with. If the spout is too short, the water will fall onto or near the horizontal surface (called the deck) around the basin, instead of in the basin center.

CENTERSET LAV SETS have a 4-inch spread, meaning that the distance from the center of one handle to the center of the other is 4 inches. The two handles and spout are often connected on a base. This set is useful with a small basin, but it's not as elegant looking as a widespread lav set. You may see the phrase **MINI-WIDESPREAD** lavatory set; this is a centerset in which the handles and spout are not connected on a base.

WIDESPREAD LAV SETS generally have an 8-inch spread, though a 12-inch spread is not uncommon. A widespread lav set is more elegant than a centerset lav set (see above), which has just a 4-inch spread and often all of the pieces connected on a base.

SHOWER CONTROLS mix the hot and cold water and open the flow of water to the shower-head or tub spout. The trim is what is visible to the eye; concealed behind the wall is the shower valve that regulates the water flow. Usually the trim is placed 48 inches from the floor to the center, but the height can vary.

SHOWER VALVES are antiscald devices that work in conjunction with shower controls and are mandated by building codes in many states—they are a good idea even if they aren't required. There are two types of shower valve. **PRESSURE-BALANCED VALVES** prevent scalding or cold blasts by sensing sudden changes in the water pressure and adjusting the supply of water accordingly. The trim for a pressure-balanced valve typically has one handle that controls both the water pressure and the temperature. **THERMOSTATIC VALVES** maintain a set temperature and water pressure level as they mix hot and cold water. The trim of a thermostatic valve usually has separate settings for temperature and water pressure. Besides protecting against burns, anti-scald valves prevent accidents that may happen when a bather scrambles out of the way as the water temperature rockets or plummets.

SHOWERHEADS deliver water for a shower in a variety of sprays, from misty to massaging. A federal standard in effect since the mid-1990s mandates that showerheads should not deliver more than 2.5 gallons of water per minute. So-called "low-flow" showerheads further economize on the rate of water flow, which translates to savings on water and energy bills. Some showerheads have aerators that add air to the flow to conserve water. Others are designed especially for houses with low water pressure.

The standard height for mounting a showerhead is approximately 72 to 74 inches from the floor. However, this can be changed according to preference; a taller person may want a showerhead to be higher. Some showerheads have an adjustable height, which is convenient where there's a big height differential among the people using the shower.

Showerheads are often sold separately from the **SHOWER ARM,** which is the piece that is fixed to the wall that the showerhead screws into. Buying a new showerhead can be a quick and easy improvement to a bathroom; the shower arm will most likely stay the same. However, larger showerheads may require a special shower arm.

RAIN SHOWERHEADS have a broad surface for delivering water that makes it seem as if you are standing out in a rain shower. They come in a variety of styles: some are mounted to the ceiling, while others have an L-shaped shower arm that mounts on the wall. This type of showerhead requires decent water pressure to work well.

TUB SPOUTS, also known as **TUB FILLERS,** are what water flows through to fill a bathtub. The water flow is adjusted by the bathtub or shower control, or by the faucet handles, depending on the configuration. Tub spouts can run from the incredibly ornate, finished with gold and shaped like swans with intricate detailing, to basic chrome spouts (as pictured here). Some have diverter valves that control the flow of water between the spout and showerhead.

Floor and wall coverings for bathrooms need to hold up in a damp environment, and there are numerous options. For the walls, glazed ceramic tiles are traditionally installed, either from floor to ceiling or just on the lower section. On the walls, paint is commonplace, and can be stenciled with a pattern for added interest.

Unglazed porcelain tiles are a common choice for the bathroom floor. One cost-effective selection for the floor is 2-by-2-inch ceramic tile, which comes in mats that are relatively easy to install. Stone is a timeless choice for the floor and walls. Slabs of marble on the floor and walls would be a classic, beautiful, but quite expensive selection for a bathroom. Vinyl floor tiles are an economical option. Rubber flooring comes in a variety of patterns and colors and is an interesting idea. A concrete floor in a bathroom lends itself to a modern look and could be painted or have pigment added to make it any color. For an attractive as well as environmentally friendly option, choose tiles made with recycled glass. Below is a look at some of the possibilities in greater detail:

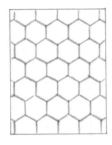

HEXAGONAL FLOOR TILES are a classic bathroom floor covering often made with unglazed porcelain. Hexagonal tiles of 1-inch diameter were used frequently in early–twentieth-century bathrooms. One-inch white hexagonal floor tiles installed with the larger white glazed ceramic subway tiles on the walls provide a period look. Tiles also come in 2- or 3-inch hexagons (or bigger), which should be considered for a spacious bathroom, where a larger scale would be more appropriate. Tiles are sold in sheets, so they do not have to be placed individually in the floor.

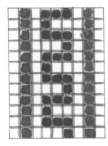

MOSAIC TILES are a modern take on an ancient art form. Historically, mosaics were pictorial wall, floor, or ceiling decoration, and their individual pieces ranged from gold to stone, glass, shell, or semiprecious stones. This was a luxurious and expensive form of decoration. The Byzantines were masters of the form and created stunning mosaics that can still be seen today in cities such as Istanbul, Turkey, and Ravenna, Italy. In the twentieth century, artists such as Marc Chagall and Diego Rivera put a modern spin on mosaics.

Needless to say, while the use of mosaic on a bathroom floor and walls is not in the same category as these works of high art, it can be very attractive. Unlike the irregular tiles of historic mosaics, contemporary mosaic tiles created for utilitarian uses are often a single color and of a uniform shape and size. Contemporary mosaic tiles also come in sheets, so that not every piece has to be laid individually. Some mosaic tiles have classic designs that work on either the floor or walls. The tiles might be ceramic, glass, or stone.

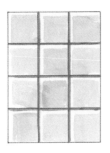

SQUARE CERAMIC TILES that are approximately 4 ¼ by 4 ¼ inches are a standard bathroom wall or floor covering. These square tiles are available in other sizes as well, and in a wide variety of colors. They can be ordered with a gloss or matte finish. Only ceramic tiles made for use on the floor should be installed on the floor. For added interest, tiles may be installed on the diagonal, so that they are diamond shaped. **FIELD TILES** cover the bulk of the wall, and they are often used along with **BORDER TILES,** which run around the perimeter or at chair-rail height (approximately 32 inches from the floor).

SUBWAY TILES are glazed ceramic tiles that measure 3 by 6 inches. They provide a classic look for bathroom, kitchen, or laundry room walls. A wall can be covered entirely in this tile, from floor to ceiling, or just the lower half. In a kitchen, the backsplash (the vertical area above the counter) is a good spot for subway tile. White subway tile was used in bathrooms during the early twentieth century and so it contributes to a period look.

TERRAZZO was a feature of twentieth-century Modern design for flooring and is often found in commercial buildings. It is traditionally made by pouring cement mixed with stone or glass chips onto the floor. The mixture is allowed to harden and then is polished down to a smooth, shiny surface. Pigments can also be added to the cement, and the size of the stone or glass pieces can be varied. Terrazzo tiles are available, as well as terrazzo products made with recycled glass.

WALLPAPER can give a bathroom a distinctive look, adding character and charm. Instead of plain old paint, wallpaper brings pattern and an array of color to the walls. In a bathroom, wallpaper may become a maintenance issue, as the steam and wetness can make the edges curl over time. If you do wallpaper a bathroom, get an extra roll or two from the same dye lot in case you need to put new paper up. The best bathrooms for wallpaper are those that are infrequently used for showers or baths, such as powder rooms or half bathrooms.

WALL-TO-WALL CARPETING can be used on bathroom floors and is particularly popular in Europe. While carpeting can look cozy, it's important to have it "laid loose and bound" so that it can be picked up and cleaned every so often. This means that it isn't glued or tacked down, as is normal for most wall-to-wall carpeting installations. Instead, the installer cuts it around fixtures and binds it so that it fits the room like wall-to-wall carpeting. Choose something with low pile instead of high shaggy pile for a bathroom, as it will be much easier to keep clean. Avoid carpeting made with natural fibers such as sisal and jute, which are rough on bare feet and won't wear well in a bathroom.

WOOD FLOORS are a favorite for the bathroom. The wood gives the room warmth and a sense of style. Wood floors in bathrooms were much more common in older houses than they are today. The wood can be painted or stained and should be finished with polyurethane. Water damage to wood floors in a bathroom is often a concern, but if water is mopped up and not left to sit, it shouldn't be a problem. Some wear is inevitable, and the wood can be recoated with polyurethane if necessary. A wood floor is a particularly good choice for a powder room, as there's less worry of water being splashed around.

Lavatory, also called **LAV** or **BASIN,** is the correct word for a bathroom sink. Traditionally, the word "sink" is not used for fixtures in the bathroom. The word "lavatory" is derived from the Latin word *lavare,* meaning "to wash"; a lavatory or basin is for bathing, while a sink is reserved for utilitarian purposes in the kitchen or laundry room. This distinction is made in construction documents and is important to know. This said, many catalogues, architects, and designers use "bathroom sink," particularly when it's a freestanding style such as a console or pedestal sink.

Most lavatories that appear to be freestanding are actually attached to the wall for support. This is because they are heavy, and the pedestal or legs alone aren't strong enough to hold them up. For this purpose, there will typically be reinforcements in the wall that the lavatory can be screwed into. A lavatory will have one, two, three, or more openings cut into it for fittings, which is the lavatory set (also called the faucet set). The number of holes and the distance between

UNDERMOUNT VERSUS DROP-IN

UNDERMOUNT   DROP-IN

There are primarily two ways to install sinks, basins, and bathtubs. **UNDERMOUNT** installation has the sink or bathtub secured under a countertop or horizontal surface. With this installation, the cross section of the countertop is visible and must be finished. Solid materials such as stone, concrete, or solid synthetics are best suited for this. Undermount installation has a modern, sleek look that is often seen in contemporary design.

A fixture, such as a sink or a bathtub, that will be installed undermount should be ordered ahead, so that a template for the size of the opening on the countertop can be made from the fixture itself. This makes for the neatest installation. Every fixture varies slightly in size, and the cut must be exact. The more accurate the opening in the countertop, the better the final product will look.

DROP-IN, also called **SELF-RIMMING,** fixtures have a lip around the top that rests on a support, such as a countertop. The installation for drop-in sinks and bathtubs is easier than for undermount fixtures, because any imperfections are concealed by the lip. One disadvantage is that the lip on a drop-in kitchen sink rises above the plane of the countertop, making it difficult to sweep crumbs into the sink; that said, a stainless steel drop-in sink is often used in a kitchen.

them determine which fittings can be used. Some lavatories have no openings, in which case the faucet is mounted on the wall or set into the countertop. There are five basic types of lavatory—console, countertop, above-counter (or vessel), pedestal, and wall-mounted—and they come in a variety of materials, including aluminum, brass, cast glass, cast iron, copper, nickel, stainless steel, stone, or vitreous china. Vitreous china—earthenware with a smooth, durable glazing—is the most common material for bathroom basins; toilets are typically made of it. Vitreous china is easy to clean and comes in a variety of colors, but it will crack if something heavy is dropped on it.

CONSOLE LAVATORIES, typically called **CONSOLE SINKS** or **WASHSTAND SINKS,** have two or four legs and exposed pipes below the basin. Some styles have integral towel bars on the sides to make up for the lack of storage space below. It's a classic sink that works well in either a powder room or a master bathroom. Depending on the design of the sink itself, this style can be used in a contemporary or a retro setting; to complete a retro look, consider white subway tiles on the walls and 1-inch white hexagonal unglazed porcelain floor tiles.

COUNTERTOP LAVATORIES are supported by a vanity. They can be set into a countertop with either an **UNDERMOUNT** or **DROP-IN INSTALLATION,** or they can sit above the countertop (see below).

ABOVE-COUNTER LAVATORIES, also called **VESSEL LAVATORIES,** rest on top of a counter, revealing the shape and design of the bowl. They are made in many different styles and materials, but in general they have a contemporary look and can be a focal point in a bathroom. The lavatory set can be either deck mounted, or wall mounted; however, this style of basin lends itself to wall-mounted fittings.

PEDESTAL LAVATORIES, often called **PEDESTAL SINKS,** have a stand, or pedestal, that covers the plumbing lines below the basin.

While it appears that the pedestal supports the full weight of the sink, in most cases it must also be secured to the wall and will likely require additional support within the wall. The look may be old-fashioned or contemporary, depending on the material and style of the sink. In a tight space, a pedestal sink is a good option, as it takes up little floor space. However, since there's no room under the sink for storage, as there is with a vanity, it's important to plan where towels and bathroom supplies will be stored.

WALL-MOUNTED LAVATORIES are bolted to the wall, so there are no legs and no pedestal. Sometimes a cover fits over the drainpipes; it's a matter of preference whether you want to conceal the pipes or not. In a tiny bathroom, a wall-mounted basin takes up no floor space, which means you can put a wastepaper basket underneath it. Some come with a shelf unit that fits underneath, which can be helpful. Wall-mounted basins are used in handicapped bathrooms, as they allow a person in a wheelchair to get closer to the sink than would be possible if there were legs or a pedestal.

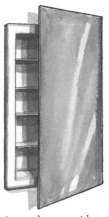

Medicine cabinets add valuable storage space to a bathroom. Typically, they are placed above a basin and have a mirrored door. They can be recessed into the wall, so that the doors are flush, or almost flush, with the wall, or they can be mounted onto the wall. Note that walls must have a certain depth to hold a recessed medicine cabinet, so it is not always possible to install one. Also, if there are electrical boxes or pipes in the wall above the basin, this might limit the size of the medicine cabinet that can be recessed. The type of door is another consideration. Sliding doors on a medicine cabinet may prove annoying, as you can never see everything in the cabinet at once; a hinged door, or a pair of hinged doors, makes surveying the contents much easier.

In the 1930s, there was a fashion for tall, narrow cabinets recessed into a bathroom wall. This can be useful in addition to, or instead of, a medicine cabinet. The cabinet can be recessed by a carpenter into a pocket between the studs in the wall; it would be approximately 4 inches deep, less than 16 inches wide, and could extend from above the baseboard to as high as you can reach.

Replacing a tired medicine cabinet can spruce up a bathroom. If the new recessed medicine cabinet matches the size of the old one, including the depth, this shouldn't require much work. It's possible to install a larger cabinet, but this will be more labor intensive.

Instead of a medicine cabinet, just a mirror can be hung on the wall and storage can be found elsewhere. A half bathroom or a powder room, for example, probably won't need the storage space that a medicine cabinet provides.

Mirrors are an important part of any bathroom design. Typically, there is a mirror over the basin, either on the door of a medicine cabinet or hung independently on the wall. In a half bathroom or powder room that isn't used for everyday bathing, a mirror without a medicine cabinet is probably all that is needed. For a formal powder room, a mirror with a rather decorative frame is a good option.

A full-length mirror is useful in a bathroom and can be installed directly onto the wall or the back of a door; a glazier will supply the mirror, cut it to the correct size, and install it. Be sure at least a few feet of open space exists in front of the mirror, so that you can step back and take in the entire head-to-toe view. A glamorous 1940s-esque bathroom might have a mirror installed over the entire wall. Just remember that if two walls facing each other are mirrored, you will see yourself replicated for eternity.

Partitions can be added in a bathroom to separate the toilet from the rest of the room, allowing some privacy if two people are using the room at once. A partition may extend from the floor to the ceiling, or just halfway to the ceiling. If it stops midway, the top will need to be finished with a smooth surface. A basic partition is not difficult to build; it will be approximately 4 inches thick, which is the width of the wall studs. A partition may also be built with materials such as glass blocks or panels of etched glass; both of these allow some light through, which can be quite nice.

Powder rooms have a toilet and a basin but no bath or shower. The term is essentially a fancy way to describe a half bathroom intended for guests to use. The powder room is usually on the first floor of a house near the living room, dining room, or kitchen, and so is a part of the more public and decorated space in a house. A powder room can be a great opportunity to use wild and wonderful wallpaper—something that might be too bright or too busy for a larger space. Generally, wallpaper with a relatively small-scale design works best, since the room is small. A small crystal chandelier or interesting hanging fixture can be very stylish in a powder room, although wall-mounted light fixtures over the basin may provide enough light. Think about hanging a framed print or two on the walls and, if there's a window, a pretty window treatment such as shutters or a bamboo or fabric shade. A powder room also provides an opportunity to incorporate a basin in an interesting material, such as metal, stone, or glass.

Saunas are a dry heat bath in which stones are warmed to raise the temperature in a small enclosed space and then water is thrown on the hot rocks to generate steam. The sauna was thought to originate in ancient Rome, when heated stones were doused with water to create steam in the public baths. Today, the sauna is a part of everyday life in Finland; there, the practice is to beat your skin with branches while in the sauna and then to exit and dive into icy water. Similar customs are also found in the Turkish hammam and the Native American sweat lodge, which have all been touted for their health benefits.

A sauna can be installed in or near a bathroom. It is traditionally lined in spruce or pine and has benches at different levels, with the air around the highest levels being hotter. The heater typically runs on electricity, though if electricity is not available a wood burning heater will do. The water is usually brought into the sauna in a bucket and a ladle is used to throw water onto the heated stones. Prefabricated modular units can be ordered, or a sauna can be custom built. People with circulatory system issues or who could be pregnant should check with a doctor before settling into the sauna for a cleansing roast.

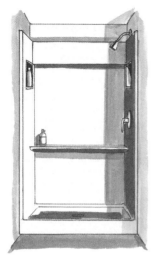

Showers can be separate enclosed units, or simply a showerhead over a bathtub. If at all possible, it's best to have a separate shower enclosure and bathtub. For the elderly, a separate shower is safer, as it means not having to step over the side of a tub to get in and out. A separate shower can also have a seat, which provides comfort and safety, for example for leg shaving. Of course, when it's not possible to have a separate shower enclosure, a showerhead over a bathtub gets the job done.

A shower has three parts: the shower floor with a drain, the walls surrounding the shower, and the shower door or curtain on a pole at the entry. These components can be prefabricated or custom-made. The shower floor can be made of acrylic, stone slabs, stone tile, ceramic tile, or glass tile. The shower walls can be made with any water resistant material suitable for installation on a wall—from ceramic tile to stone slabs to fiberglass wall panels. The following describes installation options and components in more detail:

ALCOVE INSTALLATIONS feature a shower or bathtub that is enclosed by three walls. The fourth wall has either a shower curtain or a door that hinges outward. When purchasing a shower floor, the models offer one threshold, double thresholds, or an angled threshold; a shower floor for an alcove installation would have one threshold, as there's only one side open.

CORNER INSTALLATION for a shower means that it's set into a corner, so that two sides are against walls and the other two are open (see opposite). For

a corner installation, the shower floor requires a double threshold or an angled threshold, since there are two sides that are open. These open sides are covered by a shower curtain or shower doors.

SHOWER BODY refers to the supply pipe and shower valve, an antiscald device, which are concealed behind the wall. (See p. 142 for more information on shower valves.) The components of the shower body that are hidden within the wall are called the rough, and the other elements that are visible—such as the tub spout, showerhead, and shower controls—are known as the finish, or trim.

SHOWER CURTAINS are used for a bathtub that doubles as a shower or for a shower enclosure. They come in a myriad of styles, and can be a single sheet of plastic or, for a more sophisticated choice, made of fabric protected by a plastic liner. In this case, the plastic liner can be scrubbed and eventually replaced if it gets moldy. To prevent a shower curtain from getting moldy, keep it fully extended after a shower so it can dry out; if it is left pushed over to one side, the water won't easily evaporate from the folds. The **SHOWER CURTAIN POLE** is typically installed approximately 6 feet from the floor. It's a good idea to measure the length of the shower curtain you'd like to use first and take that measurement into consideration when installing a new shower curtain pole.

SLIDING BATH DOORS are mounted on a track along the top edge of a bathtub to create an enclosed space for a shower. This is typically done when the bathtub is installed in an alcove with three walls surrounding it; the sliding doors act as a fourth wall. An alternative to sliding bath doors is to hang a shower curtain on a rod, which may look more stylish than some older textured plastic sliding bath doors. If you're looking for a simple bathroom makeover, consider taking out old textured sliding doors and putting in a shower curtain instead. A glass door that hinges is another attractive option, but keep in mind that a hinging door requires space to swing open.

Steam baths have been lauded for their detoxifying and cleansing properties for centuries. A good steam bath opens the pores and conditions the sinuses; anyone who has had a facial knows that steaming is integral to cleaning the pores. While a hot shower can act as a steam bath of sorts, for a true spalike experience an actual steam bath can be installed into a shower enclosure or a separate enclosure. A steam bath requires a water supply line and an electrical outlet, and it's a good idea to ask a knowledgeable contractor and the manufacturer of the steam bath about ways to avoid any potential moisture or mold problems that could be brought on by the steam. If you have any circulation or health issues or could be pregnant, check with a doctor before stepping into a steam bath.

Toilets, also called **WATER CLOSETS,** are available in a variety of styles and designs. Sixteenth-century Englishman Sir John Harington is credited with inventing one of the first modern-day flush toilets, which he installed in Queen Elizabeth's palace at Richmond, Surrey; the toilet had a tank of water for flushing and was connected directly to the cesspool. (Harington was, supposedly, later banished from the palace after publishing an off-color essay about the queen's toilet.) The mid- to late eighteenth century saw improvements to toilet design that kept sewer gases from rising back up into the room. In England in the 1870s, a man named Thomas Twyford developed the first ceramic toilet, a model very similar to what is still commonly used today.

Toilets previously required many gallons of water per flush, but since the mid-1990s it's been federally mandated that only 1.6 gallons of water be used per flush. The toilets that meet this requirement are known as low-consumption toilets. Older houses, however, often still have toilets that expend more than 1.6 gallons of water per flush.

There are two types of toilet flushing systems: **GRAVITY-FED** and **PRESSURE-ASSIST.** Gravity-fed toilets use the force of gravity to pull the water down from the tank to flush the bowl. This method is generally the quieter of the two. Pressure-assisted toilets store water in a sealed tank under pressure; when the trip lever is activated, the water comes out very fast and forcefully. Pressure-assisted toilets use a **FLUSHOMETER VALVE,** and are sometimes described as having a flushometer flushing system. This type of toilet conserves water; owners may be eligible for tax credits.

Toilet seat height is something to consider. For people with disabilities, the federal Americans with Disabilities Act recom-

TOILET SHAPES

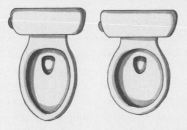

ELONGATED TOILETS have a bowl that is longer and more oval shaped than a round front toilet. It usually measures 18 1/2 inches or more from the front of the seat to the bolts holding the seat down— about 2 inches longer than a round front toilet. In residential design, it's a matter of preference, and of available space, whether you choose an elongated or a round front toilet.

ROUND FRONT TOILETS have less depth than elongated toilets. The bowl is 16 1/2 inches or less from the front to the bolts for the seat. In a tight space, a round front toilet saves a few inches.

mends that toilets be 17 to 19 inches from the top of the seat to the floor. A toilet with a bowl rim height of 16 1/8 inches or higher will usually meet this requirement once the seat is installed. Some people find lower toilets to be more comfortable, though, and there are models available with 15-inch or lower rim heights. Any toilet you choose will only need a cold water supply line. Toilet seats and trip levers, which are the levers you push to initiate a flush, are sometimes sold separately. The following are some examples of toilets you're likely to see today.

COMPOSTING TOILETS have an enclosed tank to facilitate aerobic decomposition of waste. They use little to no water and are not hooked into a municipal sewer system or a local septic system. There are different types, but in general they all break down the waste, so that the end result can be used as fertilizer. These toilets can be used in areas where a septic system isn't working correctly or can't be installed; they are also an option for houses designed for minimal environmental impact. Some models have heating units and air vents to facilitate the composting process. There are issues of capacity, so it's important to figure out which type best suits your needs. Also,

before installing a composting toilet, check local building codes to learn what, if any, regulations are in effect.

HIGH-TANK TOILETS, also called **PULL-CHAIN TOILETS,** are Victorian-era toilets in which the tank is raised high above the bowl and a pull chain initiates the flush. New reproductions of this style are available that conform to low-consumption regulations. If you are trying to create an authentic Victorian look, a high-tank toilet lends itself to this purpose. The tanks come in wood and with ceramic finishes; natural dark wood is typical of Victorian furnishings.

ONE-PIECE TOILETS have a tank and bowl constructed out of one continuous piece, most typically vitreous china. They have a lower profile than the two-piece toilet, where a separate tank and bowl are bolted together. One-piece toilets have a modern look and are thought to be easy to clean because the surface area is smooth, with few contours and spaces between elements. This is the best option if there are space constraints in the bathroom, or if you like the modern look. In addition, some one-piece toilets connect to drainpipes in the wall instead of the floor, which might make them a more viable option for certain situations.

TWO-PIECE TOILETS have a separate tank and bowl, which are bolted together. The two-piece toilet is the traditional standard; it is typically bigger and less expensive than a one-piece toilet.

WALL-MOUNTED TOILETS have no pedestal base and are supported by the wall. These are often found in handicapped-accessible bathrooms. If it is necessary to have a toilet connect to drainpipes in the wall instead of the floor, this model is ideal.

Vanities are bathroom cabinets with a basin installed in the countertop and storage space below. For storage, it's best for a vanity to have a combination of drawers and shelves behind doors. A clothes hamper built into a vanity is an excellent use of space.

Vanities come in many styles and sizes—from ultramodern to traditional, and from very small to quite big, with two basins and loads of counter space—and they can be custom-made. The countertop can be any water-resistant material, from stone to a laminate; the options are as varied as those for kitchen counters (see p. 108). The look you're after and your budget will determine the materials and style.

Be sure to leave enough space between a vanity and other fixtures for a wastepaper basket and to make cleaning easy. Typically, a vanity is 32 to 34 inches high and 22 to 24 inches deep, although taller people may prefer a higher one. When buying a vanity, be sure to check what is included with it, since items such as the basin and countertop may need to be purchased separately.

The term vanity also may be used to refer to an antique dressing table. This antique form has no basin or plumbing, and instead is a very feminine essential for a dressing room.

WASHSTANDS have two or four legs and a countertop with a basin set into it. Originally, an antique washstand was meant to hold a bowl or small tub of water that was carried to and from it. A washstand is similar to a vanity, and the two terms are sometimes used interchangeably. However, a vanity has enclosed storage space below the basin, whereas a washstand does not. Some antique washstands can be converted into modern working ones; a hole has to be cut into the top for the basin and the plumbing lines connected. This can make a pretty addition to a traditional bathroom.

vital systems

7

LIKE A LIVING ORGANISM, a building has vital systems that are essential for it to function properly. These include the electrical and gas systems, heating, ventilation, and air-conditioning (referred to as HVAC), and plumbing; they have evolved over hundreds of years to make houses more comfortable than ever before.

When buying a new house, it's critical to have an inspector review all of these systems. You must know before buying if the systems are adequate to meet your needs, or if they will need to be upgraded. In general, it's a good idea to have a basic vocabulary and understanding of the internal workings of your house, should anything go wrong and need repairing or replacing. And when installing or upgrading new systems in a house, energy efficiency is an important consideration and you should be aware of the options.

The systems in a building are a complicated matter. What follows is a basic rundown:

Electrical systems in buildings power everything from kitchen appliances to security systems to lighting. It's easy to take electricity for granted—until there's a blackout and everything grinds to a halt.

Typically, electricity is generated in a plant and travels from the plant to transformers, which lower the voltage to a level that smaller distribution systems and buildings can handle. The electricity then enters a local distribution system, which can be either underground or above ground on power poles. From the distribution system, two 110-volt wires and one "neutral" wire are run to a house. A household today typically requires 220 volts to support the appliances that have become commonplace. An older house might only have one 110-volt wire running to it; this is something to check when buying a house, since upgrading the electrical system will be a significant capital improvement. The wires connect to the house, run through a meter where the utility company measures electricity consumption, and then links to the main panel. From the main panel, electricity is distributed by branch circuits throughout the house.

Electricity that is generated by burning coal or other fossil fuels creates a lot of pollution. Cleaner alternative methods of generating electricity include solar and wind power, fuel cells, and hydropower. It's possible to buy electricity from your power company that is generated using cleaner alternative methods. It might be a bit more expensive but is well worth looking into.

Local building codes dictate what can be done with the electrical system in a house. A licensed electrician will be familiar with the local regulations and can advise when a building permit is necessary.

CIRCUIT BREAKERS cut the flow of electricity when a circuit gets overloaded and there's too much power flowing through it. Shutting down the circuit prevents a potentially dangerous situation. Each branch circuit in a building has a circuit breaker; older houses or buildings constructed before the 1960s often have fuses instead. Circuit breakers and fuses have the same function, but are designed differently. A circuit breaker is more convenient, as it simply has a switch that can be flipped, unlike a fuse, which must be replaced when it blows.

Circuit breakers and fuses are rated according to the size of the circuit they monitor: if a circuit breaker is rated for 20 amps, it will switch off if there are more than 20 amps going through it. If a circuit breaker trips and shuts down a circuit, for example when a hair dryer overloads the system, you can locate the circuit breaker and flip it back on. If this is an ongoing problem, you should have an electrician look at it. Sometimes, especially in an apartment building, smaller subpanels service a particular section of a building.

ELECTRICAL BRANCH CIRCUITS carry electric current from the source of electricity, which is a main panel or a smaller subpanel, to electrical outlets and back to the source. There needs to be a full circuit, or circular path, for the current to flow. For instance, when a light switch is turned on, the hot and neutral wires that make up the circuit are connected to complete the path. Electricity flows down the hot wire to the electrical outlet and back to the source over the neutral wire. The hot and the neutral wires are separated, breaking the flow, when the switch is turned off again.

One circuit can feed electricity either to a group of outlets or just one outlet, which is called a dedicated outlet. Circuits are 110 volt or 220 volt; 220-volt circuits are typical for appliances such as an electric stove or air conditioner. Newer houses have grounding wires in the circuits, which protect against shocks. Older houses might not have any grounding wires; this is evident if all the outlets accept only two-prong plugs.

FUSES are devices that stop an electric current from overloading a circuit. A thin strip of metal running across the fuse literally "blows" when this occurs, and the fuse then has to be replaced. Fuses are found in the main panel or smaller subpanels, which are also sometimes called fuse boxes. Since the 1960s, they have been replaced by circuit breakers. Both are rated for the amount of current they allow before shutting the circuit down; a 15- or 20-amp fuse is typical for regular use for light fixtures, for example. It's critical for safety and convenience that a fuse be the correct rating for a circuit. If a fuse is rated too low for the circuit, it will keep blowing out; if the rating is too high, the fuse will allow too much electricity into the circuit, which can cause a fire.

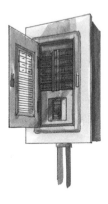

The **MAIN PANEL** is usually located near where the electric power enters a building, and is where all the circuits in the house originate. It is also the location of the main circuit breaker that turns off the power to the whole system in a building. If there's a problem with the main panel—for example, if fuses are blowing—it's best to call an electrician to check it. Sometimes smaller subpanels, also called branch panels, serve a particular area, such as an apartment or

ROUGH IN is a term used for plumbing and electrical system installations. Roughing in refers to the installation of the pipes and wires that will be concealed in a wall after the process is complete. A building inspector checks the pipes or wires after they have been roughed in but before the walls have been closed. At this time, it's a good idea to double-check that the pipes and outlets are where you want them to be.

a wing of the house. Both the main panel and subpanels have either circuit breakers or fuses, which serve the same function of shutting off overloaded electrical circuits. Fuses are typically found only in older houses.

The main panel has a rating that determines the total amount of current that can flow out to the circuits at one time before the main circuit breaker shuts the system down. Most moderately sized older houses have 100-amp service; some smaller ones have 60-amp service. In many cases this is adequate, but larger new houses tend to have main panels that handle 200 amps to accommodate all the electronic gear used these days. If you're doing construction work in an older house, consider upgrading the electrical system and increasing the total amps that can come into the house. This is a worthwhile improvement that can increase the resale value of a house: if you or a potential buyer wanted to build an addition to the house, or add more appliances, the electric power would be there for it.

OUTLETS are the receptacle for plugs that provide electricity to a lamp or an appliance. There are a few different kinds of outlets; some accommodate plugs only with two prongs, and others take plugs with three prongs. The third prong on a plug connects to the circuit's grounding wire. Older houses that haven't had their electrical systems upgraded might only have two-prong outlets, and no grounding wire in the circuits. **DEDICATED OUTLETS** have an entire circuit, with a circuit breaker, to themselves. They are generally required for air conditioners, and for larger appliances such as washing machines and dryers.

GFI OUTLETS, which stands for **GROUND FAULT INTERRUPTER,** are required by the building code when installing an electrical outlet near a water source or in a damp location. This type of outlet, common in a bathroom, has two buttons—one that reads "test" and the other "reset." Regular circuit breakers or fuses cut the electricity flow when a circuit is overloaded, but they don't protect against a ground fault. This occurs when electricity leaves its intended path and aims to be grounded elsewhere. Water, as well as the metal of plumbing fittings, conducts electricity, making the bathroom or kitchen particularly dangerous for ground faults. The GFI quickly detects electricity gone astray and cuts the power. Since the 1970s, GFIs have been required in certain situations by building codes, for example kitchen appliances must have GFI outlets as well as outlets near kitchen sinks. GFI outlets are also known as GFCI, or ground fault circuit interrupter.

THREE-PRONG OUTLETS have a grounding wire, which is what the round third prong on a plug connects to. A grounding wire protects against electric current escaping from the circuit and causing shocks. Older houses might have only two-prong outlets; besides not providing grounding protection, this can be problematic if an electric item has a three-prong plug. Three-prong outlets can be installed without the grounding wire, but this doesn't provide the protection that such an outlet should offer. Upgrading the electrical system to include grounding wires requires opening the walls, and this means a considerable amount of work. There are adapters that can be plugged into a

two-prong outlet so that a three-prong plug will work. Some of these offer grounding protection with a wire that attaches to the screw in the outlet's cover plate.

TWO-PRONG OUTLETS are found in older houses that don't have an upgraded electrical system with grounding wires in the circuits. If you live in an old house or are thinking of buying one, it makes sense to look into updating the electrical system to ensure that it's as safe as possible. This can also be a good capital improvement.

Gas systems bring gas into a building for various uses, including heating, cooking, or for a water heater. Natural gas is the most common type used. It is extracted from deep inside the earth, like oil, refined, and then delivered through a utility company's gas pipelines to a building and routed as needed throughout. Natural gas in its original form is colorless, odorless, and combustible; the familiar odor we know is added so that leaks can be detected. Not all buildings have access to natural gas pipelines, in which case other gases or fuels are relied upon. Propane, butane, or another type of gas may be used instead of natural gas, and these are typically stored onsite in tanks.

HVAC stands for heating, ventilation, and air-conditioning and is a critical building system. An HVAC system can include a furnace or boiler, air ducts or steam pipes, radiant heating elements, central air-conditioning, and ventilation systems such as bathroom and kitchen exhaust fans, which all work to create pleasant temperatures and humidity levels.

In designing an HVAC system, noisy equipment should be kept away from quiet spaces like bedrooms—you don't want to hear the furnace clanging into action in the middle of the night. Also, it's important to change filters and do routine maintenance on HVAC systems as recommended by manufacturers. With a hot air heating system, this will help to minimize air pollution in the house by filtering out dust and mold in the air ducts.

AIR-CONDITIONING controls air temperature and humidity within an interior space. It is based on the same technology by which a refrigerator functions: coolant runs in a loop, absorbing heat from the inside of a space and releasing it outside of the enclosed area. Air-conditioning also removes humidity from the air, which helps make it feel cooler.

Window air-conditioning units are versatile but ugly. They block the view out of a window and are distracting to look at from the exterior. Double-hung windows, which have two sashes that slide vertically, lend themselves to a window air-conditioning unit, whereas

NATURAL COOLING

Before the advent of air-conditioning, a house had to be kept cool by design. Root cellars are one option; they have been used for ages for storing fruits and vegetables. They are built into the ground where, at a depth of 10 feet and more, the earth is a constant 50 to 55 degrees. Above ground, kitchens were typically placed on the the north side of the house since it is the coolest, and featured cool closets for storing food.

Structural elements such as cupolas and skylights can work to release heat from a room; since heat rises, it can flow right out of such openings. In warm climates, low and long eaves are built to shade interiors from direct sunlight. Planting can also shield windows from too much sun.

casement windows, which hinge like a door, do not. Through-wall air conditioners are like window units, but they are installed directly through an exterior wall, usually under a window. They require a sleeve, which goes around the air conditioning unit and helps to secure it in the opening of the wall. Both window and through-wall air conditioners cool just the areas around them in a house. A central air-conditioning system cools the entire building, or specific zones within the building.

With any type of air-conditioning unit, it's important to get the correct size. Air conditioners are rated by Btus, which stands for British thermal units. The higher the Btu rating, the more cooling power the air conditioner has. Talk to an expert about your requirements for cooling a specific area. Air conditioners also have a SEER, or an EER, rating; SEER stands for seasonal energy efficiency ratio, and EER for the same thing minus the "seasonal." EER ratings are used for individual room units, and SEER ratings are for central air-conditioning systems. The higher the rating number, the more energy efficient the air conditioner is. A SEER rating of 13 or more is considered energy efficient for a central air system, and an EER rating of 10 is relatively efficient for an individual unit. This is likely to change as standards are upgraded and air conditioners become more efficient.

CENTRAL AIR-CONDITIONING is a big-ticket item, but one that can increase a house's resale value. Air-conditioning first appeared in the early twentieth century, and by the 1950s it had become popular for residential use. Newer construction today, especially in warmer climates, commonly has central air-conditioning; older houses and buildings in cooler climates might not, but it's possible to add it.

If a house has a forced air heating system, with a furnace that heats air and distributes it via air ducts throughout the house, then an air-conditioning system can piggyback onto the heating system. This typically requires installing a compressor and condenser unit outside of the house and an evaporator unit indoors near the furnace.

If a building uses a boiler for heat, or something other than a forced hot air system, no air ducts will be in place. To add central air-conditioning in this case, the air ducts need to be installed, which can entail lowering the ceiling in places and running ducts through the basement and attic spaces and into the rooms. There are mini-duct air-conditioning systems that make this installation easier.

HEATING is a necessity for any dwelling outside of the tropics. Without it, the building's water pipes—not to mention the inhabitants—would freeze. The earliest heating system was an open fire; it was smoky and unhealthy. The ancient Romans developed what is thought to be the first central heating system, called the hypocaust system, in which an open space below floors acted like an air duct, allowing hot air from a fire to flow through and heat the floor and room above. With the decline of the Roman Empire, the open fire came back into vogue. Much later, a well-known heat source for houses was the Franklin stove, invented by Benjamin Franklin in the 1740s. This wood-burning stove provided direct heat and was widely used through the eighteenth and nineteenth centuries. Steam heat came into use in the nineteenth century. By the twentieth century in the United States, hot water and hot air systems were commonplace.

In a cold climate, heating can account for a major portion of the energy bills, so it pays to be as efficient as possible. Economy of energy can be achieved by turning the heat down (which is better for furniture and the wood inside the house, anyway), by plugging up any gaps that let in cold air, and through choosing systems that are efficient. Oil, natural gas, and electricity are three common fuels for heating. Some cities, such as New York, have high-pressure steam systems for heating as well, where the steam is distributed by utility companies. There are many ways to heat a house, including passive solar systems (see p. 181), and some heating systems are used in conjunction with cooling and ventilation systems. A few heating system basics are outlined below:

BOILERS heat water as part of a hot water or steam heating system. The hot water, or steam, is distributed from the boiler through pipes to radiators, or other heating elements, which give off the heat and warm the space. The cooled water then returns to the boiler to be reheated again. A boiler is typically fueled by natural gas, fuel oil, or propane. Natural gas is piped in as needed, whereas fuel oil and propane are usually delivered by truck and stored in a tank. Fuel oil and propane must be paid for in advance, unlike natural gas, where you pay as you use it. Older boilers were fueled by coal, which created ashes that had to be swept away. In general, a boiler will be kept when improving or restoring an older house, as water pipes take up less space than air ducts and installing ducts requires opening walls and may compromise the architecture of the house. Some boilers are Energy Star rated, which means they are particularly energy efficient.

Fin tube baseboard convectors run along the baseboard and have vertical "fins" that distribute the heat. Air is drawn in, warmed over the fins, and blown out the top of the unit. The fins are heated by hot water from the boiler.

Radiators are heated by hot water or steam. Cast-iron radiators are typically placed under a window in every room to be heated. Modern designs for radiators take up less space and look more stylish than the older, clunkier models. One benefit to cast-iron radiators is that they retain heat. A radiator can complicate a furniture layout, though, as it takes up space and it's best to avoid putting a piece of furniture right up against it. A radiant heating system is an alternative, in which the heating pipes are installed into the floors and walls and do not interfere with furniture layout.

ELECTRIC RESISTANCE HEATING relies on electricity to heat a space. This type of heating has either a forced air furnace that runs on electricity and supplies heat to many rooms at once or else individual heaters for specific rooms. Electric baseboard heating units are one type of individual heaters; they have coils heated with electricity.

Electric heating units can also be installed on a wall or recessed into the floor. Radiant heat that uses electric cables in the floors is also a type of electric resistance heating. Individual electric heating units are something to consider if you're adding on a room and don't want to run the existing heating system into the new space. Electricity is usually a more expensive option than oil or natural gas for heat.

FURNACES heat air for a heating system, and are a common alternative to hot water heating systems using a boiler. A fan or blower pushes the warmed air from the furnace through ducts and into the rooms. A thermostat works to start and stop the warm air and maintain a steady room temperature. This form of heating has become a widespread in the United States and is used in most new construction. Furnaces are typically fueled with natural gas, propane, or oil. As with boilers, the natural gas is piped in as needed, whereas oil and propane have to be delivered and stored in a tank.

Hot air systems have filters in them to clean the air; these should be maintained as recommended by the manufacturer. It's possible to have a central air-conditioning system work in conjunction with a hot air system, using the air ducts to deliver cool air. Furnaces come in a number of types and models; the heating requirements as well as other factors will determine which is best for the job.

GEOTHERMAL HEATING AND COOLING SYSTEMS are considered particularly energy efficient and environmentally friendly. Below the ground surface, the earth retains a steady temperature of about 50 to 55 degrees. In the winter, a geothermal heating and cooling system collects heat from underground, compresses it to increase the temperature, and distributes warm air throughout the house. In the summer, this process can be reversed to cool a building. This system can also heat a hot water tank. Tax credits are usually available for a geothermal heating and cooling system, since it is so energy efficient.

HEAT PUMPS can be used for both heating and cooling and are known to be energy efficient. A heat pump uses coolant and a small amount of electricity to move heat from one place to another. There are different models, but one common type is an air-source heat pump that brings heat from the outside air into the house in the winter and in the summer is reversed to expel warm air from inside the house. When collecting air from outside the house, the device concentrates the heat, so that the air it pumps in is warmer than that outside. Heat pumps work best in moderate climates; in cold climates, they are less efficient. It's possible to qualify for tax credits for installing a heat pump.

RADIANT HEATING warms the floors, and sometimes the walls and ceilings, so that they radiate heat. These energy-efficient systems have metal or plastic pipes with warm water circulating through them embedded in the floors, walls, or ceiling. The water may be heated by a boiler, an active solar system using a solar collector, or a heat pump, for example. It's also possible to have an electric system, in which heating cables are placed inside the floor, walls, or ceiling. A benefit to radiant heating is that it is completely concealed under the floor; meaning there are no heating elements, such as radiators, which will interfere with a furniture plan. However, one drawback is that it takes a relatively long time for a space to heat up.

VENTILATION is typically required by building codes in places such as over a cooktop or in a bathroom with no windows. It is essential for expelling moisture and odors from the air inside a house.

Exhaust fans come in different strengths, and it's important to have the right size for a particular room. They are graded according to the number of cubic feet per minute (CFM) of air that they draw out of the room. Exhaust fans are also rated by how loud they are in "sones," a measure of sound output; the lower the number of sones, the quieter the fan. Many bathroom exhaust fans are between one and four sones, with one being very quiet and four being quite loud. Check with the local building department or an HVAC (heating, ventilation, and air-conditioning) expert on the local requirements before installing a ventilation system. In an apartment building, there may be regulations about running ducting for a ventilation system, so inquire first before beginning work.

BATHROOM EXHAUST FANS draw the air from a bathroom through ducting to the exterior of the building. Bathrooms have high levels of moisture, so an exhaust fan is required to prevent mold and mildew. This is true of all bathrooms, but in particular those that don't have windows. For an approximate guideline on what size fan to buy, the cubic feet per minute (CFM) rating should match or slightly exceed the square footage of the bathroom; for example, a 90-square-foot bathroom would require a 90 to 100 CFM exhaust fan. If the ceiling height is greater than 8 feet, a higher CFM rating is suggested. It's a good idea to talk with an expert about what your bathroom requires.

Some exhaust fans come equipped with lights, heaters, and even nightlights. In a renovation or new construction, keep in mind that it's nice to be able to turn a light on in the bathroom without also switching on the fan.

KITCHEN VENTING SYSTEMS draw heat, steam, and cooking fumes out of the kitchen through a duct. Some models filter and then recirculate the air, and these are known as ductless. However, it's more effective to expel the exhaust through the exterior of the building. A kitchen ventilation system typically includes a hood installed over a cooktop or range. There are also downdraft vents that pull air down into a range or cooktop unit instead of up through a separate venting hood. These vents have ducting like a regular venting hood. Appliances such as microwaves sometimes have built-in ventilation systems, so they can be installed over a cooktop or range; this is an option in a tight space.

Plumbing is the system of pipes that carry water and liquid waste through a house. The word is derived from the Latin word *plumbum*, meaning lead. In ancient Rome, lead pipes were part of the Romans' advanced plumbing systems; today, pipes are usually made of cast iron, copper, or a plastic material.

Fresh water for residential use comes from a municipal water system or, in rural areas, a well. The source of water is either groundwater from aquifers, which are geological formations that hold water deep underground, or surface water from reservoirs, rivers, and lakes. The wastewater from a house empties into either a septic system in rural areas or a municipal water treatment facility. Both systems remove solid wastes and then purify and release the water back into nature to start the cycle again. Toxic chemicals aren't necessarily removed from the water during this process, and therefore shouldn't be flushed down drains, as they will pollute future "fresh" water.

When buying a house or moving into a place where the water is drawn from a well, have it tested for pollutants. With municipal water supplies, chlorine is usually added to prevent the growth of bacteria, and the water is regularly tested and monitored.

Plumbing codes dictate much of what can (and can't) be done within a plumbing system. Before undertaking any project that alters the plumbing, find out if you need a building permit. An architect, general contractor, or plumber should know what the local requirements are.

There are two basic types of pipes: supply lines, which bring fresh water to a fixture such as a sink; and drain- or waste pipes, which take dirty water away. A **MAIN** is a major pipe; a **RISER** is a vertical pipe; and the **SHUTOFF VALVE** turns off the water supply. You should know where the main shutoff valve of the house is in case of an emergency. The following are a few basic components of a plumbing system:

The **DRAIN WASTE VENT SYSTEM** encompasses all the pipes that are not supply lines. These pipes flush wastewater out of the house. They are wider in diameter than supply pipes and usually are made out of cast iron or a plastic material such as PVC (short for polyvinyl chloride). Using gravity, drainpipes run from appliances and fixtures such as toilets, sinks, and showers down to a municipal sewer line or septic system. Vent pipes have air in them and are often vertical extensions of drainpipes that merge into one or more vent stacks on the roof. These pipes allow sewer gases to escape through an opening in the roof, instead of rising up through drains in the house; they also prevent wastewater from getting stuck in the plumbing lines. Imagine a straw filled with water: you can stop the water from flowing out of the straw by covering the top opening with your finger. Similarly, air that vent pipes bring into the plumbing system prevents such suction from occurring.

PIPES used to be made with lead, which some have said contributed to the decline of the Roman Empire by making its denizens crazy from lead poisoning. Lead plumbing is still occasionally found in buildings today, especially in older ones. (Water can be tested to check the lead levels, and filters can reduce the amount of lead in water.) If a house has plumbing materials with lead in them, it's recommended, especially for children, to use cold water for drinking and cooking, and to run water from the tap for a few minutes before consuming it. (For more information on lead see p. 187). Building codes will dictate what materials can be used for supply pipes. Copper is widely used as it lasts a long time and resists corrosion, though it is quite expensive.

HARD WATER VERSUS SOFT WATER

Hard water has minerals such as calcium and magnesium in it, which can leave deposits in the pipes, known as scaling, and make soap practically ineffective. With hard water, soap won't bubble, and it won't easily wash out of your hair or clothes. The hardness of water varies from area to area, and well water is most likely to have this problem. One solution to this is water softeners. The first water softener company was launched in the 1920s and became a big success. A water softener can be added to a plumbing system; water is run through a small tank in which the minerals are removed using an ion exchange process. With softened water, soap will foam and pipes are saved from mineral deposits.

PEX, made with cross-linked polyethylene, is also used for supply pipes. It is gaining in popularity and is used in green design. Previously, galvanized iron was used for supply pipes, but it was replaced by copper when it became clear that galvanized iron corrodes over time. For older buildings that may still have galvanized iron pipes, signs of corrosion include low water pressure and bits of rust in the water; eventually, these pipes will need to be replaced. Supply pipes inside a building are much narrower than drainpipes, typically about ½ an inch to 1 inch in diameter, depending on their purpose.

For drain and vent pipes, PVC, ABS plastic (which stands for Acrylonitrile-Butadiene-Styrene), and cast iron are common. Cast iron is durable, relatively expensive, and labor intensive to install; it also muffles sound better than plastics. PVC and ABS plastic have little soundproofing ability so you'll hear the waste running down the pipes in the walls from a bathroom. Sometimes cast iron waste pipes are used in walls just around public rooms in a house instead of plastic pipes to minimize noise. This is something to discuss with an architect, general contractor, or plumber if you're doing new construction or renovating. PVC and ABS plastic waste pipes are avoided in green design. Alternatives are pipes made with cast iron, vitrified clay (usually used for sewer or larger applications), and polyolefin plastic.

SEPTIC SYSTEMS are installed when there is no municipal waste system. Wastewater from the house goes into a septic tank via a sewage line. Inside the tank, the sewage decomposes over time and then is released into a leaching zone on the property, most likely in the yard. Anything that doesn't decompose sinks to the bottom of the tank— which is why it should be pumped out once a year. When buying a house with septic tank, find out when it was last pumped and how old the system is. Before doing any new construction in an area with no municipal waste system, look into whether and where a septic system can be built on the property.

TRAPS are the curved drainpipe under a fixture such as a sink. The trap holds standing water, which prevents sewer gases from floating up out of the drainpipes. If there were no traps, the sewer gases would bring unpleasant odors into the bathrooms and kitchens. There will always be a trap under a plumbing fixture, though it is often concealed in a vanity or under a counter. In a toilet, the trap is below the bowl. Usually water in the trap is refreshed; if a fixture isn't used for a long time, the water in the trap can evaporate and the sewer gases will rise up into the room. All traps connect to a drain line and a vent line. Remember, if you drop something valuable like an earring down the drain not to run the water; with any luck it will get caught in the trap, instead of heading right into the sewer system.

VENT PIPES are part of a house's drain waste vent system. They allow air into the drainage system to prevent wastewater from being siphoned back up the pipes and also permit sewer gases to exit the building. A vent system terminates in one or more outlets on the roof of a building. Vent pipes can be vertical or horizontal. When moving fixtures like bathtubs and sinks, the vent pipes have to be considered along with the drain and supply pipes.

WASTE PIPES carry water away from fixtures such as sinks and bathtubs. When renovating a bathroom, take into consideration that moving waste pipes involves quite a lot of work. New fixtures like basins can be put onto the old pipes, but moving the pipes entails construction. At the base of a vertical waste pipe, typically there is a **CLEANOUT**, which can be opened to provide access for clearing clogs.

WATER HAMMER is the pounding, hammering, or banging of a pipe that occurs after you shut off the water. This is caused by a sudden surge of pressure that sends shock waves ringing down the pipe; for instance, when water is rushing toward the open faucet and it is suddenly shut off, the water under pressure slams into the closed valve. Water hammer can damage pipes and fittings. Devices called **WATER HAMMER ARRESTERS** fit onto supply pipes to help stop the banging.

WATER HEATERS can operate in a few different ways, and when choosing a new one take energy efficiency into consideration, since a large portion of the average household's energy consumption goes toward heating water. A water heater with a **STORAGE TANK,** the most popular type, holds approximately 20 to 80 gallons of water and keeps the water hot all the time. While these storage tanks have become increasingly energy efficient and can be further insulated to conserve energy, they consume energy just maintaining the temperature in the tank. **DEMAND WATER HEATERS,** also called **TANKLESS WATER HEATERS** (pictured here), are an alternative in which water is heated as needed and not stored hot. This saves energy, and thus money, since heat won't be lost through the storage tank; they are also typically a larger investment upfront than a water heater with a tank. **HEAT PUMP WATER HEATERS** work on the same principle as the heat pump (see p. 168). These can be very efficient, by harnessing the naturally occurring heat from the outdoors to heat water. **INDIRECT WATER HEATERS** are also typically energy efficient; they make use of the existing boiler or furnace to heat the water. Another particularly efficient alternative is a **SOLAR WATER HEATER.** Like any solar power equipment, this involves an upfront expense followed by savings over time as water is heated for free. In colder climates, a solar system will probably need to be backed up by another system to heat the water, but can still significantly reduce heating bills.

When choosing a new water heater, consult an expert about the correct size for your needs. Also, a water heater that burns oil or gas will have to be vented properly to run safely. To save energy, hot water pipes can be insulated, and the temperature on the heater can be lowered. If you move to a house with an old water heater, it may be worth it to invest in a new, more efficient one. Hot water pumps can be installed on sinks and showers that pump the hot water to the tap before it starts flowing; this saves quite a bit of water, as it eliminates the need to run water while it heats up.

WATER PRESSURE is measured in psi, which stands for pounds per square inch. Residential rates for water pressure fall between 40 and 80 psi. Low water pressure can be caused by a blockage in the supply pipes. This blockage may be in a localized area—near a sink, for example—or in a main pipe. A plumber can help to figure out if there's a clog and how to fix it. It's possible for pipes to become clogged with rust or minerals. If the water pressure in a house is too low, a booster pump can be a solution; conversely, if water pressure is too high for a plumbing system, it can be lowered with a pressure-reducing valve. There are also showerheads specially designed for houses with low water pressure.

WELLS are holes drilled into the earth to access water (or oil, or natural gas). If a house or building is not hooked into a public water supply system, a well is needed to supply water. Wells come in three types: dug, driven, and drilled. A dug well is not very deep and will often be quite old; these wells were typically dug by hand, and the person digging would stop when water began filling the hole faster than he could bail it out. Because they are quite shallow, they can dry up if there's a drought or if the water table drops. Driven wells are made in soft ground, gravel, or sandstone, and are deeper than a dug well. A drilled well goes through bedrock to a water source hundreds of feet below the surface. It typically has a pump at the bottom, whereas dug or driven wells will have pumps inside the house or at the top of the well.

Wells should be maintained regularly; the water should be tested annually and a well contractor brought in to inspect it for problems. The water in wells can become contaminated, particularly in more shallow ones where surface runoff water can easily infiltrate them. Wells should also be kept at recommended distances from septic systems, livestock yards, petroleum tanks, and other potential sources of contamination. If you're buying land with the idea of building and there's no public water supply, first make sure that you'll be able to install a well that will provide enough water. Also keep in mind that the well pump relies on electricity to work; if there's a power outage, you could run out of water, so a backup generator is a good idea.

APPENDIX A: GREEN DESIGN

GREEN DESIGN AIMS TO CONSERVE ENERGY, minimize water consumption, use renewable materials, and improve indoor air quality. As we continue to hear about global warming, greenhouses gases, diminishing supplies of fresh water, and increasing pollution everywhere—including in our houses—it's important to realize that the choices we make as individuals always contribute to a larger whole, for better or worse. Making green choices can lead to reduced utility bills and a healthier living environment, and may be eligible for government incentives. Building green can cost more upfront, but this has to be weighed against future energy and money savings and the overall benefits to society and the environment.

Electricity is expensive, and generating it with coal or oil creates a lot of pollution. Besides turning off the lights when not in use, there are choices you can make to cut down on your electricity consumption. Appliances, as well as heating and cooling systems, that bear Energy Star labels have been flagged by the U.S. Department of Energy and the U.S. Environmental Protection Agency as being particularly energy efficient; look for the label when you are considering a new purchase. Taking maximum advantage of natural light and using the right amount of insulation also helps to reduce energy use. Solar power is a green option for at least a portion of household electricity requirements, such as heating a hot water tank.

Some architects, developers, and general contractors focus on green design, and there are retail stores that specialize in green products and materials. Green design in large part is implemented during the design and construction of new buildings and in renovations. For someone who is just sprucing up, decorating, and not embarking on a major project, eco-friendly considerations can be made in the choice of surface materials and furnishings—from carpeting and paint to appliances and cleaning supplies. The U.S. Green Building Council has green guidelines and a host of resources and information on the subject on its website: www.usgbc.org. Some green design basics include the following:

Gray water is wastewater that comes from sinks, showers, and bathtubs. It is distinguished from the water that comes from toilets, which is known as black water. Gray water systems recycle and filter this water for reuse within a house for purposes such as irrigation and flushing toilets. However, local building codes vary on whether they allow gray water systems.

Green materials are nontoxic to people and the environment. Many adhesives, types of plywood, paints, insulation, and other building materials have VOCs, which stands for volatile organic compounds. These compounds are easily released into the air—called outgassing or off-gassing—for a period of time. The smell of a new car, new wall-to-wall carpeting, freshly dry-cleaned clothes, or a wet coat of paint is really the smell of VOCs. The green choice is to use materials with low or no VOC emissions, to keep the air inside a house as clean and healthy as possible.

When considering materials, remember that locally manufactured, grown, or quarried materials require less energy to transport to the job site. A rule of thumb for green design is to buy materials that come from within a 500-mile radius of the building project.

Materials with recycled content require fewer resources to manufacture; products such as floor tiles, gypsum wallboard, and certain brands and types of insulation are made with recycled materials. Salvaged architectural elements and building materials also use less energy than all-new ones. Green design considerations also focus on materials that will eventually decompose or be recycled, and thus not still be floating around a landfill one thousand years from now; for example, wood will eventually decompose, but some synthetic materials will not. The following are some natural materials that are considered green:

BAMBOO, a type of grass that grows all over the world, is environmentally friendly because it grows quickly: depending on the species, it can grow a foot or more per day. This means that fewer resources are consumed in growing bamboo than in cultivating large trees. Bamboo is used to make furniture and build houses, and its shoots are even eaten in Chinese cuisine. Bamboo flooring looks much like a hardwood floor and is a durable choice. For building projects, there is plywood made of bamboo instead of wood.

CORK comes from the bark of the cork oak tree, *Quercus suber*, found in the Mediterranean region; Portugal in particular has historically been a major producer of cork. A cork oak tree does not have to be cut down to harvest the cork; instead, layers of the bark are removed. Eventually, the bark grows back, thus making it a renewable resource. Cork is known for its excellent soundproofing properties and is frequently used as a flooring material in libraries. A cork bulletin board can be installed over an entire wall, which is a great way to display photographs and such.

LINOLEUM is made with natural ingredients and is an old favorite for kitchen and bathroom floors. It consists of linseed oil, powdered wood, ground limestone, resins, and pigments, a recipe that was patented by Englishman Frederick Walton in 1863. When shopping for linoleum, take care to distinguish between true linoleum and vinyl sheeting, which has been marketed as linoleum but which is not a green choice. Linoleum requires occasional polishing and can be stripped to remove built-up polish or caked dirt; find out what type of maintenance and which products are recommended for specific linoleum products.

MILK PAINT is concocted using buttermilk, crushed limestone, and natural pigments. It's been around for hundreds of years and comes in rich historical colors. Milk paint can be applied on furniture or walls, but it needs to be sealed with a wax or oil if used on furniture or areas likely to get wet. Milk paint has no VOCs. Alternatively, there are other paints made by well-known brands that have low VOC emissions.

STONE is, to state the obvious, a natural product that lasts for a long time. In architecture and interior design, stone can be used for walls, floors, exterior veneers, and countertops, to name a few options. Choosing local stone or salvaged stone for a building project saves energy.

WHEATBOARD is made of wheat straw and like particleboard is used as a base for cabinetwork. However, wheatboard is the more green choice over particleboard, because wheat straw is a renewable resource and the adhesive used to manufacture wheatboard is free of formaldehyde. Kitchen cabinets can be constructed of wheatboard with a veneer of wood.

WOOD products are a green choice if they are harvested using responsible practices, or if they are made from reclaimed wood that is being reused. Some wood products are certified by the Forest Stewardship Council, which ensures that responsible logging has been followed. More information about the Forest Stewardship Council can be found at www.fscus.com.

$LEED^{®}$ which stands for Leadership in Energy and Environmental Design, is a green design rating system developed by the U.S. Green Building Council. LEED ratings offer a standard measurement of how green a building is and apply to commercial as well as residential buildings. There are now multiple types of LEED rating systems and more in development. They include: LEED-NC (new commercial construction), LEED-EB (existing buildings), LEED-CI (commercial interiors), LEED-CS (core and shell projects), LEED-H (homes), and LEED-ND (neighborhood development). More information about LEED ratings can be found at www.usgbc.org/leed.

Low-emissivity glass, also known as **LOW-E GLASS,** has a coating that allows light to enter a room but prevents heat from escaping. It is added to windows and doors with glass panels to con-serve energy. Windows typically have double or even triple glazing for insulation purposes, meaning that there are two or three pieces of glass in a single window unit. Low-emissivity glass adds additional energy efficiency to any window whether it has double or triple layers of glass. While low-e windows can be more expensive, the money you save in fuel efficiency should make them worthwhile.

Rain catchment systems collect rainwater for use in a house or building. This may be as simple as a barrel left under a gutter down spout, or it can be a sophisticated system with large storage tanks. As green design becomes more mainstream, building codes are changing to accommodate this. Before installing a large scale rain catchment system, however, it's best to check local codes.

Solar energy can be utilized to heat a house and also to generate electricity. The two most obvious benefits are that sunlight is free and doesn't create pollution. Taking maximum advantage of solar energy is clearly a green choice. There are a few different ways to harness solar energy, as follows:

ACTIVE SOLAR SYSTEMS have solar collector panels that absorb and store energy from the sun, which is then used to heat a house or simply a water tank. This system is different from a solar electrical system, which has photovoltaic panels to convert sunlight into electricity. Both systems are green choices, but they serve different purposes. An active solar system uses either liquid or air to absorb the sun's heat inside a solar collector. The warmed liquid or air is then circulated and distributed through the house, or stored for later use. An air solar system may augment a forced air heating system, where air is warmed by a furnace and distributed via ducts through the house. A liquid solar system can be used for radiant heating, in which narrow pipes run through floors, or the walls and ceilings, and heat a room. Active solar systems reduce energy costs and can complement a solar electrical system, which generates electricity.

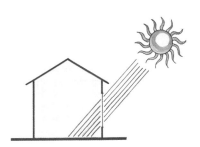

PASSIVE SOLAR SYSTEMS use the design of a house itself to store the sun's heat. This may be done, for example, with windows on the south-facing wall of a building that allow in lots of sunlight; this sunlight warms a floor made of stone or concrete that will hold the heat and release it slowly. The size of the windows should be a certain percentage of the size of the floor, and the window glass (also called glazing) needs to be a specific type. This method is known as direct gain passive solar design. The ability of a material to absorb heat energy is called thermal mass; concrete and stone, for example, have a high thermal mass and so are ideal for use in passive solar design.

Another method of passive solar design is to have an exterior wall made of a material with a high thermal mass. There may be tubes of water inside the wall, which absorbs the heat and releases it into the interior of the space; this kind of a setup is known as indirect gain. Another form of indirect gain is to have a roof pool—literally a shallow pool on the roof—which retains heat and releases it into the room below.

SOLAR ELECTRICAL SYSTEMS have photovoltaic cells that convert the energy in sunlight into electric energy. Solar cells are linked to form modules, and these modules are connected to form arrays, a grouping of modules. The amount of electricity generated depends on the geographical location of the house and the size of the system. In the United States, the southwest is the sunniest part of the country, but solar electrical systems can be effective in many other locations.

A solar electrical system can be connected to a utility company's distribution system, or it may be an off-grid, stand-alone system. When connected to the utility's distribution system, backup electricity is available if the solar system doesn't produce enough to meet the needs of the household. In addition, if the solar electrical system is making more electricity than is required, the extra energy is sold back to the utility company. This is called **NET METERING,** and it means you are paid for the extra electricity generated. Stand-alone systems make sense if you live in a place where it is prohibitively expensive to bring in power from the utility, or if your solar system is meant for a small application, such as outdoor lighting.

A solar electrical system needs to be installed so that it gets direct sunlight. In some situations, there might not be enough space on or around a house to support a system of solar panels; a less conspicuous alternative is photovoltaic shingles, which can be installed on a roof.

An initial upfront cost is required for the system, but this should be recouped over time in saved utility bills and net-metering proceeds. Check local building codes before installing a solar electrical system, and consult an expert in the field who can calculate your energy needs and design the best system for your requirements.

GREEN ITEMS MENTIONED ELSEWHERE IN THE BOOK

COMPOSTING TOILETS (see p. 155)
FIBER CEMENT SIDING (see p. 25)
FLUSHOMETER TOILETS (see p. 154)
GEOTHERMAL HEATING AND COOLING (see p. 168)
HEAT PUMPS (see p. 168)
METAL ROOFS (see p. 19)
PAPER-BASED KITCHEN COUNTERS (see p. 112)
SOLAR WATER HEATERS (see p. 174)

Vegetated roofs, also known as a **GREEN ROOFS,** have been planted with grasses, or even plants such as wild strawberries. The vegetation and soil help to mitigate water runoff after a storm and keep the roof cool. An added benefit is that a green roof can be prettier to look at than a plain old black roof. Forms of vegetated roofs have been around for hundreds, even thousands, of years for similar reasons. If you are considering this option, keep in mind that the roof structure must be able to support the weight and must have the proper drainage. There are people who specialize in constructing vegetated roofs.

Wind power systems generally are seen in large-scale applications such as wind farms, where hundreds of whirling propellers produce clean electricity. The wind spins the rotors on the turbine, which in turn spins a small generator that makes electricity. It's possible to produce electricity at home using wind power, but this is contingent upon having ample space for the wind turbine (as well as a steady amount of wind). Like a solar electrical system, a wind power system can be connected to a municipal utility's distribution system, or it can stand alone off the electrical grid. The advantages of connecting to the grid are the same as well: municipal electricity can be used if the wind system doesn't meet your needs, and any extra power generated can be sold back to the utility (this is called **NET METERING**). Wind power systems can be used in conjunction with solar electrical systems to generate power more consistently. A wind system also requires an initial investment upfront that should pay off over time. Local zoning regulations must be checked before installing a wind turbine.

BESIDES LOCKING THE FRONT DOOR at night, there are a number of steps you can take to make sure your house is a safe place to live. Some basic safety precautions, such as installing carbon monoxide detectors and maintaining chimneys, are easy to do and may help prevent a disaster.

As with any safety equipment, remember to always follow the manufacturer's suggestions about how to install and operate it. And for more information regarding hazardous substances that may be found in a house, like asbestos, lead, and radon, see the Environmental Protection Agency's website: www.epa.gov. The following are some general home safety issues:

Asbestos is a naturally occurring fire-resistant mineral that has been mined since the nineteenth century. In particular, it has been used in insulation, roofing shingles, vinyl sheeting, vinyl floor tiles, and a number of other building materials that benefit from being fire resistant. Unfortunately, a few decades ago it was proven that inhaling asbestos particles can lead to deadly lung disease and cancer.

When you're buying a house or apartment, it can be checked for asbestos as part of the building inspection. Asbestos is problematic primarily when it's disturbed and particles become airborne, or "friable." Before ripping up vinyl floor tiles made before the 1980s or letting your kids shoot hockey pucks into the boiler insulation, it's a good idea to have asbestos testing done. Some products are labeled, but if you are unsure, it's best to have it checked.

If asbestos is found in your house, it's generally recommended that you leave it alone unless the building material is damaged or you plan to renovate or otherwise agitate it. Having asbestos doesn't automatically mean you need to remove it; building codes vary from municipality to municipality on how to handle asbestos. However, asbestos remediation can be an unforeseen cost in a building project.

Carbon monoxide detectors are required by law in

some locations. Even when they aren't required, it's a good idea to install them. Carbon monoxide is a by-product of combustion, and at high levels it can be poisonous, even deadly. When inhaled, carbon monoxide attaches to a person's red blood cells instead of oxygen, so that breathing it in essentially suffocates you. Symptoms of carbon monoxide poisoning are headache, nausea, dizziness, and feeling like you have the flu. Since you can't see, smell, or taste carbon monoxide, a detector is necessary to alert you to a dangerous situation.

Gas and oil-burning furnaces, water heaters, and appliances produce carbon monoxide, as do wood-burning fireplaces, charcoal grills, and cars. If ventilation systems or chimneys are not working correctly, carbon monoxide levels can increase to dangerous levels inside a building. An essential preventative measure is to make sure all chimneys, vents, and heating systems are regularly maintained.

It is recommended that detectors be placed high on the wall, or even on the ceiling. The most important place to install one is near where you sleep, so that you will be woken up if the alarm goes off. Having one detector on each level of a residence as well as outside of all the bedrooms is recommended. Detectors that only plug in, without a battery-powered backup, will not work if the power goes out. It should also be noted that carbon monoxide detectors are different from smoke detectors; having one does not eliminate the need for the other.

Proper chimney maintenance is vital in preventing

chimney fires and carbon monoxide buildup in a house. In addition to wood-burning stoves and fireplaces, oil- and gas-burning furnaces (and boilers) also have chimneys. It is recommended that each chimney be cleaned and inspected once a year, and even more frequently if it gets a lot of use. Have all the chimneys cleaned and inspected when you move into a new house.

A chimney sweep cleans a chimney and inspects it for damage. Cleaning is necessary to remove soot and creosote, which is a combustible residue that results from burning wood, in particular green wood. In addition, birds and animals often make nests in a chimney, or leaves can accumulate, and these blockages can be responsible for a chimney not working correctly. As with hiring anyone else, when choosing a chimney sweep, get someone who is experienced, insured, and who comes well recommended.

Fire extinguishers are rated in four different classes: class A is used to put out ordinary combustibles, such as wood and paper fires; class B extinguishes flammable liquids, such as oil and grease fires; class C is for electrical fires; and class D works on flammable metals. It's critical to choose the correct class for a particular situation. Some fire extinguishers can extinguish several different types of fires, and so have multiple ratings; these will, for instance, work on both ordinary combustibles and flammable liquids. A fire extinguisher with multiple ratings is best for general use in a house.

It's a smart idea to have at least one fire extinguisher in the house. The kitchen, areas near the furnace, workrooms, and garages are all places likely to have a fire. If in doubt about what type of fire extinguisher to get, how to use it, or where in the house to keep it, ask your local fire department for advice.

Lead is a metal that has been used in paint, plumbing materials, and as an additive in gasoline, among other things. When ingested, lead can cause a host of horrible health problems, including brain damage, behavioral and learning problems, and high blood pressure, to name a few. Some of the ways people can get elevated lead levels are by eating paint chips or soil with lead in it, by breathing lead dust, or by putting their hand or an object with lead dust on it into their mouths. Children and adults can be tested for lead levels in their bodies. It's a good idea to know if you have lead in your house and to be aware of the potential hazards and options for dealing with it.

In 1978, the federal government mandated that lead paint could no longer be used in houses. This means that a house built after 1978 is not likely to have lead paint, but chances are that an older house does. Lead paint that is peeling or chipping can be hazardous, but if it is in good condition, it isn't as dangerous. Sanding and scraping old lead paint is a sure way to generate lead dust in a house; this is something best left to an expert.

Lead in a house may also come from soil contaminated through paint or from gasoline spills (back when lead was still commonly used in gasoline), which is tracked into a house on shoes. A building and the soil around it can be tested for lead, and for remediation it's important to work with someone experienced in removing and dealing with lead.

Pipes and some plumbing fittings might have lead in them as well. This is not usually considered as hazardous as other exposures to lead, but is something to be aware of. Water in a house can be tested for lead and steps taken to lessen or eliminate lead found in the water.

Mold is a fungi that produces spores that float through the air, land on damp surfaces, and start growing. People who are allergic to mold may encounter asthma and other allergic reactions when exposed to it. Some types of mold are toxic and can cause serious health issues.

While there will always be mold spores in the air, it can become a problem when there are damp surfaces in a house for the spores to land on and multiply. Essentially, mold grows where there is moisture. Fixing leaks and using dehumidifiers, air conditioners, and exhaust vents in kitchens and bathrooms help to prevent mold from growing. The air inside a house can be tested for levels of mold spores to help determine the extent of a mold issue. If there is a serious mold problem affecting a large area of a house, such as after a flood, mold remediation by professionals should be considered. The Environmental Protection Agency's website has more information on mold: www.epa.gov.

Radon is an invisible radioactive gas or particle that enters a house through the foundation or well water and is known to cause lung cancer. When buying a new house, the inspector can test for radon. To be accurate, the test typically requires that the doors and windows of the house remain closed, with all air conditioners and vents shut off, for one day. There are different types of tests, some of which you can do yourself. If a test comes back showing a high level of radon in the house, it can be lowered relatively easily and at a reasonable expense. How the level of radon is lowered depends on the particular house, but some basic methods include sealing cracks in the foundation and installing vents and fans in the basement.

Security systems installed in a house can combine tasks and act as burglar, fire, carbon monoxide, flood, medical emergency, or low temperature alarms. The options vary greatly: some security systems are monitored by a company to which you pay a monthly fee, while some are programmed to directly alert local police or fire departments if an alarm goes off. You can set up some systems yourself, but others require professional installation. Installing a security system in a house can significantly lower homeowner's insurance premiums; it's a good idea to ask your insurance company about this.

Smoke alarms cut your risk of dying in a fire by half. Since they don't cost much and are required by law, there's every reason to have them in your house. There are two types of smoke alarms for households: photoelectric alarms use a light-sensitive cell to detect smoke; ionization alarms use a tiny amount of a radioactive substance to sense smoke. Ionized alarms detect smaller smoke particles faster than photoelectric alarms, which detect larger smoke particles faster.

It is recommended that a smoke detector be placed in all sleeping areas and on each level of a house. Because smoke rises, the alarms should be installed on ceilings or at the top of a wall. Building codes now typically mandate smoke alarms. It's important to read the manufacturer's guidelines for alarm installation and maintenance. Most alarms last about ten years and should be replaced as recommended. The battery in a smoke alarm must be regularly tested and replaced as well.

Wood-damaging insects can harm the structural integrity of a house. If you suspect that you've got an insect infestation in your house, call a pest control expert as soon as possible. Some insects, termites in particular, will do serious damage to wood and therefore the structure of a timber-frame house. If you are looking at a house to buy, the inspector should check for signs of an insect problem. In most cases, these bugs are attracted by moisture and are often found in areas where the wood from the house, such as wood siding, touches the ground. The following are some pests to watch for:

CARPENTER ANTS are relatively large (up to $\frac{1}{2}$ inch long) black ants found throughout the United States. They don't eat wood, but build nests inside wood that they hollow out. Some carpenter ants

LEFT TO RIGHT: CARPENTER ANTS, CARPENTER BEES, POWDERPOST BEETLES, TERMITES

have wings and look much like winged termites. Signs of an infestation include what looks like sawdust near wood. Moist areas in the house, such as kitchens, bathrooms, and spaces near leaks, are particularly prone to carpenter ants.

CARPENTER BEES resemble bumblebees and burrow into wood to make nests. Wood decks and roof eaves are typical places carpenter bees call home. The visible holes are about ½ inch wide, and the burrows can be quite long, extending up to a few feet.

POWDERPOST BEETLES are small (about a third of an inch or less) and come in a variety of species. The adults bore a hole into unfinished wood, and then larvae do the damage inside the wood. Signs of an infestation include borings on the floor below or near infested wood that resemble small piles of sawdust. A grouping of small round holes in wood surfaces, or seeing the small beetles themselves, is a sure indication of a problem.

TERMITES tunnel into wood and eat it for food. There are many different types of termites, some more destructive than others, and they are found across the United States. Like ants and bees, termites are social insects with colonies, a queen, soldiers, and a set hierarchy. Signs of a termite infestation include mud foraging tubes, which are narrow tubes found on foundation walls, windowsills, or structural timbers. Winged bugs swarming in or around the house are also an indication of a problem.

APPENDIX C: FINANCING

WHEN BUYING BIG-TICKET ITEMS such as a house, most people must borrow money from the bank. When you take out a mortgage, you borrow a certain amount, called the **PRINCIPAL,** and are charged a percentage of the principal as **INTEREST** on the loan. Mortgages have a specific duration; fifteen- and thirty-year mortgages are common. This means your payments are calculated so that by the end of this period, you will have paid off the loan. When the bank gives you the loan, it typically holds the **MORTGAGE,** also called a **DEED OF TRUST,** on your property, which gives it the legal right to have your property sold to pay off the debt if necessary. Mortgages and deeds of trust are a type of **LIEN,** which is a general claim against a property. The worst-case scenario is **FORECLOSURE,** which occurs when the bank takes possession of the property and sells it because the loan is not being repaid.

Typically, the interest paid on a mortgage for a primary residence is tax deductible. Property taxes paid on your primary residence may also be tax deductible. When looking at real estate to buy, it's easy to get excited about the possibilities, so keep in mind that the smaller the mortgage you need, the better. If real estate values drop in years to come, you don't want to be stuck with a property that is worth less than the amount you still owe to the bank.

The following are some of the basics about financing a property:

Amortization is paying off of a debt in installments. An amortization table shows the total number of monthly mortgage payments that must be made, as well as the breakdown of how much of each payment is interest and how much is repaying the principal. At the beginning of a mortgage, the payments are predominantly interest and little goes toward paying down the principal. Over time, this reverses. This means that if a property is sold after just a few years, very little of the amount borrowed from the bank will have been repaid.

Construction loans are short-term loans taken out to cover the cost of building a house. A bank can't issue a mortgage on a house that doesn't exist yet, so a construction loan covers the cost of building. Once the house is completed, the construction loan is usually converted to a permanent mortgage.

Energy mortgages take into account the existing or potential energy efficiency of a house. There are two types of energy mortgages. An energy-efficient mortgage is issued for a house that is already energy efficient; it takes future savings on energy bills into account and allows you to borrow more money to buy the property. An energy improvement loan helps to finance improvements that make a house more energy efficient. To be eligible for either of these, a house has to have a home energy rating done by a certified consultant. To find out more, ask at a bank or lending institution that offers energy mortgages. Besides energy mortgages, many states have low-interest loan programs to promote energy efficiency in a house or building.

Foreclosure is a legal proceeding that allows a bank to take title and possession of a property on which it has a mortgage. Once a bank does so, it may sell the property and apply the proceeds of the sale toward payment of the loan. A bank forecloses on a loan when the monthly payments are delinquent. Since the bank holds a lien, also called a mortgage or deed of trust, against the property, it has the right to sell the property to get its money back. In this case, the person who took out the mortgage will likely lose all or a portion of his own money invested in the house. If the proceeds of the foreclosure sale are not enough to pay off the loan, the bank has the right to collect the balance from the person who took out the mortgage. If you start to have trouble making payments on a mortgage, it's better to call the bank and discuss the options rather than waiting for the bank to start calling you.

Home equity lines allow you to borrow against the equity in your house. The equity is the amount the property is worth less the amount of a mortgage. With a home equity line, you get a checkbook and a line of credit for a certain amount of money—this is the maximum you can have outstanding at any one time. Like using a credit card, the checks are written against the line of credit, though the interest rate is typically much lower than credit card rates. The arrangement is flexible, in that you can increase or decrease the amount of money borrowed according to your needs and are charged interest only on the amount that is actually outstanding. If you sell the property, the home equity line is closed, and any outstanding debt has to be paid off. The process of getting a home equity line is the same as getting a mortgage, and the bank will hold a lien against the property until the line of credit is fully closed out. Home equity lines can be handy for consolidating credit card debt, for home improvements, or to pay for a family vacation. Like a mortgage, though, it's possible for a bank to foreclose on the house if payments are delinquent. So, as with any financing, a home equity line should be treated with care, as your house is at stake if the bills aren't paid. A home equity loan is similar to a home equity line, but provides a lump sum up front as a loan instead of a revolving line of credit.

Mortgage *interest rates* are the percentage at which interest is charged on a loan. Interest is a sum paid for the use of money. When you borrow money from the bank, you are paying the bank interest for the use of their money; in the case of a savings account, the bank is paying you for the use of your money. The factors influencing the general level of interest rates are a complicated matter best left to bankers and economists; in short, however, the banks set a prime interest rate that fluctuates according to a variety of factors. When the prime interest rate increases, then all interest rates tend to increase, and when the prime interest rate decreases then all interest rates tend to decrease.

Mortgages can be structured a couple of different ways. With a **FIXED INTEREST RATE,** the interest rate on a loan is locked in for the duration of the loan. If interest rates are low, this is what you want. A **FLOATING INTEREST RATE,** also called an **ADJUSTABLE RATE MORTGAGE** or a **VARIABLE RATE MORTGAGE,** will go up or down according to fluctuations in the prime interest rate or some other accepted benchmark. A floating interest loan might have a lower rate to begin with than a fixed interest loan, but there's no guarantee that the rate won't increase significantly. If interest rates are already high, then a floating interest rate can make sense, as interest rates might go down; however, there is no guarantee that they will. There are a wide variety of options, including mortgages in which the interest rate is fixed for a period of time and then reverts to an adjustable rate.

It's possible to buy "points" when taking out a mortgage, and doing this can get you a lower interest rate over the life of the loan. Buying points is a means of buying a lower interest rate on a loan. If you plan to hold on to a property longer than the national average of approximately seven years then points can save you money. If you sell your property sooner than that, then the expense of the points will typically outweigh the savings of the reduced interest rate.

Preapproval, or **PREQUALIFICATION,** for a mortgage is given

by a bank after a preliminary look at your credit report, income, and expenses. A preapproval letter from a bank says that based on the information you have provided, you may be eligible for a particular mortgage program; this program might be, for example, a thirty-year fixed-rate mortgage in the amount of $150,000 at an interest rate of 6 percent. A formal application has to be made to get approval for a mortgage, but this preapproval informs you—and anyone else who may need to know—that you are eligible to borrow a certain sum of money.

Refinancing is paying off an existing mortgage with a new

mortgage that has a lower interest rate or other more agreeable terms than the first one. When interest rates go down, homeowners often refinance.

BUYING, SELLING, OR EVEN RENTING real estate is a major event, especially if you're doing it for the first time. If you're buying a house or apartment, keep in mind the old phrase *caveat emptor*, meaning "let the buyer beware." It is not the seller's responsibility to point out problems with a property.

If a deal sounds too good to be true, then it usually is. If a property is cheap, there's a reason, and it's critical to find that out before you sign a contract of sale on the deal. Some reasons for bargain-basement prices might be that an area has just been rezoned and a four-hundred-unit condominium is about to be built next door; that it's not possible to build a septic system on the land; or that the building across the street has just been declared a toxic waste site, and so on.

When considering a property to buy, in addition to having all the systems and the structure inspected by a certified home inspector or engineer, check out the neighborhood and look into local zoning laws. If you want to buy a place because you love the view, find out if a skyscraper might soon be built to block it. Make sure any alterations you'd like to make are possible. For instance, if you're buying with the hope of eventually building an addition, you'll want to know in advance if the local zoning laws will allow it. In smaller towns, it's possible to inquire at municipal buildings in the planning and building department offices. Always act as your own best advocate by asking questions, reviewing all papers before you sign them, and checking for mistakes. A knowledgeable real estate broker and attorney can assist in gathering information about the property.

Real estate law and how transactions are handled vary from state to state—what's true in Rhode Island isn't necessarily true in Florida. A basic rundown on real estate terminology is provided below, but it's critical to ask someone familiar with local laws how exactly the process works and what the regulations are. For example, the role of the real estate broker and the real estate attorney may be different in each state.

An *acre* is a unit of measurement equaling 43,560 square feet. Land is usually measured in acres in the United States and England. For comparison, a standard American football field is 48,000 square feet (and if you are not a football fan, an acre is roughly the size of 15 ½ tennis courts placed next to each other). There are 640 acres in a square mile. It is thought that the measurement was originally derived from the area that a pair of oxen could plow in a day.

An *agreement of sale* or **CONTRACT OF SALE** is the agreement between the buyer and the seller that outlines the terms and conditions of the sale. When the contract is signed, the property is "under contract." The buyer typically has to make a down payment to secure the contract, generally about 5 to 10 percent of the final sale price. This down payment is held in an escrow account, usually by the seller's real estate attorney or real estate brokerage office. If the buyer were to walk away from the deal, in most cases the seller is entitled to the down payment.

The contract includes all the particulars of the transaction—the price, the closing date, a schedule of what appliances and fixtures are to be included or excluded, any contract contingencies, and so forth. It's a good idea to have a real estate attorney look over the contract of sale before you sign it.

A *buyer's market* is when there is an excess of properties for sale relative to demand. This gives a buyer many options, as well as room to try to negotiate the price down. Ideally, you buy a property during a buyer's market, but realistically you never know when it's going to happen. The opposite is a seller's market, during which there are an excess of buyers for the number of properties on the market; in this market, the seller can be expected to hold out for the asking price or higher.

TIPS FOR SELLING

If you're trying to sell a house or apartment, remember that clutter is a killer. When prospective buyers walk into a space, you don't want them to see piles of your personal stuff strewn around the house. Remove the clutter—one way or another—before putting a property on the market.

Taking the time to clean the windows will make a big difference in how the house shows. Dirty windows make a space seem darker and give it an overall dingy appearance. Make closets look spacious and organized by ditching old tangles of wire hangers and getting matching plastic or wood hangers. Potential buyers should be able to look into your closets and happily imagine their own clothes hanging there.

The *closing* is the final step in the sale of a property. It is when the money and the title to the property change hands. There are a variety of "closing costs." For both buyers and sellers these costs range roughly from 2 to 6 percent of the sale price, though this can vary according to the location. For a buyer these costs might include reimbursing the seller for fuel oil or propane gas left at the property, attorney's fees, title insurance, as well as fees paid to the managing agent of a building. In addition, the cost of a new mortgage may include paying for an appraisal that the bank conducts, as well as the bank's closing fees. The seller's closing costs may include attorney's fees and taxes as well as fees paid to a managing agent. Ask your attorney to estimate the closing costs in advance, to lessen what can be a nasty surprise.

A *contingency* is a provision in a contract of sale that says a specific action has to happen before the sale can be completed. A sale might be contingent on the buyer getting a mortgage, for example; if the buyer cannot obtain a mortgage (and can demonstrate that he has made a diligent effort to do so), he can typically back out of the deal without losing the down payment. In certain cities, there are cooperative buildings where a buyer must be accepted by the board of the building before the sale can be closed, and this would be a contingency in the contract.

Curb appeal is how a property looks at first glance, when potential buyers drive by and form their first impression. Strong curb appeal can do much to sell a house, which is why it's worth paying attention to the landscaping and general appearance of a property from the outside. If you're putting your house on the market, take the time to tidy up the exterior. A few pretty plants and flowers might make a big difference. For city dwellers living in apartment buildings, it's the lobby that gives a property its curb appeal. When you are buying an apartment in a building, take into consideration the appearance of the lobby and public spaces as they will be a factor when you sell. Also, if you own an apartment in a building and see that the lobby or exterior is getting shabby, it's a good idea to bring this up with the board of the building or the managing agent.

Exclusives give a real estate broker the exclusive right to sell a property. A seller signs an agreement with a real estate broker stating that for a specific period of time (usually no less than six months) that broker has the exclusive right to show the property and represent the seller and will be paid a commission equal in most instances to 5 to 6 percent of the selling price, though this can be lower in some areas. The exclusive broker, also called the listing broker, typically works with other brokerage firms to find a buyer for the property. This is called "co-broking." If a co-broker ends up finding the buyer, the exclusive broker pays that co-broker, usually one half of the commission.

An advantage to having an exclusive broker is that one person oversees all the showings and is responsible for marketing the property through print media, the internet, and so forth. An exclusive broker will take the time to become familiar with the property and its sales points, as he or she is financially motivated to do so.

The alternative to listing the property with an exclusive broker is to list it as an open listing with a number of brokerage firms. In most cases, this does not save money on the commission, but it may have an appeal if you're reluctant to be locked into a specific broker for a period of time. Also, since a broker representing the buyer does not have to split the commission with an exclusive broker, he or she may have additional motivation to bring potential buyers to the house. With an open listing, the seller has to take the time to be at the house during showings and to oversee the showing schedules. If there's an exclusive broker, he or she will do this.

Property *inspections* should be done by a licensed home inspector, or licensed engineer, and should include the entire house from top to bottom. As a buyer, it's a good idea to be at the inspection, so that you can see for yourself any issues that arise, ask questions, or bring to the inspector's attention any particular concerns. Typically, the sale of the property is contingent on the inspection; after the inspection, the buyers usually have the option to back out if there are structural issues and major problems, such as a failing foundation. The inspection report will come back with a list of issues—for example, that the oil fuel tank is old and needs to be replaced—and then the buyer and seller negotiate how to address the problems. Sometimes the sellers will put money aside for the buyer to cover the cost of some or all of the repairs, or the sellers might agree to fix some of the problems while the buyers agree to fix the rest.

Some things the inspector or engineer should attest to are: the state of the foundation; the condition of all the systems, such as electrical, plumbing, heating, and air-conditioning, and the appliances, insulation, and so forth; the age and condition of the roof; the presence or absence of moisture or mold; and the condition of the exterior. An inspection should also include a termite inspection, if there's any possibility of a termite problem.

Real estate agents and brokers will, if you're a buyer, show you properties, make offers and negotiate on your behalf, and shepherd a deal through to completion. If you are selling a property through an exclusive real estate broker, that broker will advise on the asking price after researching comparable sales in the neighborhood and be responsible for listing the property with other brokerage firms and advertising it.

Brokers and sales agents have different qualifications. Becoming a real estate broker is a tougher licensing process and allows the person to broker his or her own deals. A real estate broker either works with a firm as an associate broker or as an independent broker. A real estate agent is a sales agent working for a brokerage firm and cannot independently broker deals. Both agents and brokers earn a commission on the sale of a property, which the seller pays out of the sale price. To keep things simple, the term "broker" is used below, though the information is also true of real estate agents.

As a seller, you should be involved with your broker in setting the right asking price for your property. Review the comparables your

DOING YOUR RESEARCH

It's quite incredible that what is very often the biggest purchase of your life is made after only spending a couple of hours at a property. Before committing to buying a property, you should do all the research, or due diligence, you can. A lot of information will come from an inspection done by a licensed home inspector or licensed engineer; your real estate attorney should be helpful in gathering additional information about the property.

Before buying a property, you should ascertain that the house and foundation are structurally sound, and that there is no settling, cracking, or rot. You should also know the age and condition of all the major components, like the roof and the heating, electrical, and plumbing systems, so that you can estimate the necessary capital investments after the purchase. The inspection should provide this information; see p. 199 for more information on inspections.

If you're planning to renovate, install a pool, or build a guesthouse, it would be wise to know before you sign a contract that any zoning, wetlands, or other authority having jurisdiction over the property will allow the project to move forward. An attorney can assist with this, and in smaller towns it should be possible to visit the planning and building departments yourself to get information; see p. 12 for more on permits and zoning.

It's also a good idea to have a house tested for hazardous materials. Houses of a certain age are likely to have asbestos and lead, so knowing where these substances are and their quantity will be valuable information. Or there may be an underground oil tank on the property that could pose problems down the road; if there is an underground oil tank, it's a good idea to discuss it with your real estate attorney before committing; see "Appendix B: A Safe and Healthy House" for more information on hazardous materials.

A few other things to consider:

A **WET BASEMENT** could be prone to mold. This is something to keep in mind, especially if you have allergies to mold.

A dehumidifier will help with this problem but won't solve it completely. It's possible to test the levels of mold spores.

The **WATER SUPPLY** for a house will either be drawn from a well or from a public water supply system. If it comes from a well, you'll want to establish that the well is in good condition and supplies clean water. Wastewater from the house will either go into a septic system on the property or to a public sewage system. If there's a septic system, you'll want to make sure it's in good condition.

PROPERTY TAXES are a matter of public record. Since property taxes aren't fixed, they can go up (or possibly down, but that's rare). If there's a reassessment, it could mean that your property taxes will increase.

EXPLORE THE NEIGHBORHOOD if you're not familiar with it. Drive around at different times of the day, over the weekend, and during the week. Take a look at other houses in the immediate area. The neighboring houses will influence the value of a property, for better or for worse.

Finally, take the time before you make an offer to do as much research as you can. The property will usually still be available once you're done, and you'll be in a position to make a more informed choice.

---

broker is using—the recent sale and asking prices of similar properties in the neighborhood. If the asking price is too high, you'll almost certainly be turning off a number of potential buyers; in addition, if a property is overpriced at the outset, more often than not the price will have to be reduced over time. Ideally, as a seller you want your property marketed at the right price to attract buyers, perhaps even to find yourself in a buyer's bidding war.

A good real estate broker is knowledgeable and able to provide helpful advice. However, remember that a real estate broker only gets paid when a sale is made, so it's to his or her advantage to get the deal done.

It's possible to buy and sell property directly, without a real estate broker. The advantage of dealing directly is that the seller does not have to pay a commission to a broker and might sell at a lower price. It's financially advantageous to do a direct deal, although it isn't always possible to find a buyer on your own. Real estate brokers have built-in marketing systems as well as potential buyers coming to them; this can make it easier and more expedient for them to find a buyer. Additionally, they are familiar with real estate law, how the process works, and the local market; they can be valuable resources when buying or selling a property. But if you choose to forego this, there are websites where a property can be listed directly, such as www.forsalebyowner.com.

Real estate attorneys represent the buyer or the seller of a property for a real estate transaction. Typically, the buyer and seller each have their own attorney. A real estate attorney should be familiar with the area where the property is located, as it's important that your attorney know all the ins and outs of local laws. Since a real estate attorney is important to the process of buying or selling property, it's worth the time and effort to find someone who comes well recommended. Many have a flat fee structure for closings.

Titles are the evidence of ownership of a property. When you are selling a property, there will be a title search to confirm that you are the true owner and that no one has any liens against the property. (A lien is the legal right to hold a property or have it sold to pay off a debt—for instance, when a mortgage is taken out, the bank has a lien against your property.) In most cases, house buyers are recommended to have title insurance, which protects them if someone comes along and claims to have a stake in a property after they have become the owner.

Walk-throughs occur just before the closing, which is when the money changes hands and the sale is finalized. The walk-through typically happens the morning of the closing or the day before. It is an opportunity for the buyer to confirm that the seller has moved out and the place is "broom clean." It's also a chance for the buyer to make sure everything that was supposed to be included in the sale— such as appliances, window treatments, or doorknobs—is still there as agreed. The buyer can also check that the seller has completed any work on the house that he said he would. If a problem or an issue comes up during the walk-through, the closing might have to be delayed until it is resolved.

ABOUT THE AUTHORS

PAMELA BANKER is a leading interior designer with over 30 years of experience. Her work has been included in *Architectural Digest, House & Garden*, and a number of books on interior design.

LESLIE BANKER is a writer and decorator. She works as a designer at Pamela Banker Associates and also as a freelance writer.